THE DON'T SWEAT
STORIES

Other books by the editors of Don't Sweat Press

The Don't Sweat Affirmations
The Don't Sweat Guide for Couples
The Don't Sweat Guide for Graduates
The Don't Sweat Guide for Grandparents
The Don't Sweat Guide for Parents
The Don't Sweat Guide for Moms
The Don't Sweat Guide for Weddings
The Don't Sweat Guide to Golf
The Don't Sweat Guide to Taxes
The Don't Sweat Guide to Travel
The Don't Sweat Guide to Weight Loss

THE DON'T SWEAT
STORIES

Inspirational Anecdotes
from Those Who've Learned
How Not to Sweat It

By the Editors of Don't Sweat Press
Foreword by Richard Carlson, Ph.D.

New York

Contents

Foreword

Stories are one of the best ways that I know of to be touched by life. A good story speaks to our hearts. It can nourish the soul, make us smile, laugh, or cry. It can provide much needed perspective and deepen our wisdom.

Personally, I love to read stories. They help me reflect on the beauty of life and on the resiliency of people. Often, stories have inspired me to do things, to help people, or to look at my life a little differently. Often, a good teacher will use stories to demonstrate important points. They bring life and color to a message.

Since I wrote *Don't Sweat the Small Stuff...and It's All Small Stuff,* I have wanted to see a book of Don't Sweat stories. I am grateful to the authors of these particular stories and to the editors of Don't Sweat Press for creating this book.

The stories in this book are simple but powerful. One of the magical aspects to stories is that various people can read them and gain different insights from what they read. I suspect you will value these stories a great deal, in your own unique way.

While the details differ from story to story, the theme is, from my perspective, similar. There is, within each of them, the message that, deep down, life is a precious gift, despite any superficial evidence to the contrary. We can learn that we have the capacity to transform our problems and see life in new ways.

There's a story I've heard about two friends who were waiting in a long line out in the hot sun. After they had been waiting for hours and it was finally their turn, a man suddenly cut in front of them in line. One of the men who had been waiting started to wave his arms and clench his fists in protest. He was visibly upset and about to scold the man who had not waited his turn. Before he could say anything, however, his friend stopped him in his tracks. "Wait," he said, "look." They noticed that the man who had cut in line held a white cane, indicating that he was blind. It was an innocent mistake.

I don't know if the story is true or not. It's amazing, however, how the slightest shift in our perspective can make the difference between being annoyed or angered by something—or suddenly at peace.

My family and I were really excited to be going to Hawaii. While we were in the boarding area, the announcement was made that there was going to be an hour delay before takeoff.

By the looks on the faces of most passengers, you would have thought, "Oh no, something horrible has happened!" Almost everyone was angry or frustrated. There were looks of disgust and rage. One person blurted out that she was going to sue the airline—all because it was going to take one additional hour to get to paradise. It seemed there was a minor mechanical problem to solve.

It was one of those moments when I realized that many of the things we "sweat" really aren't that big a deal. It's not that anyone would actually like to be delayed, but then again, while all of us are subject to big and painful events in life, a flight delay certainly isn't one of them. In fact, when you think about it rationally, the appropriate response would have been one of gratitude. After all, the delay was to protect the passengers!

Of course, both before and since that day at the airport, I have had other experiences that reinforced a similar message, moments of clarity that have reminded me of the relative importance of things. Although I forget it sometimes, I've come to realize that life is far too important, short, and magical to spend it sweating the little things.

I've also heard stories from folks all across the country about similar moments of insight in their lives. Every time I do a book signing or give a talk, people approach me to tell me of the exact moment that they realized they needed to stop sweating the small stuff. I've enjoyed these conversations, and I wanted you to be able to have that same experience. This collection of stories shares these moments with you. At times these insights come about from a touching or funny experience. Other times, it's a moment of tragedy or a near miss of some kind. A friend of mine, for example, had a life-changing moment as the small plane he was traveling aboard was about to crash. Another friend was neurotic about keeping her house perfectly clean. Then she traveled to a country where the poverty broke her heart. Her perspective shifted and she had a major change of heart. When she returned, her home seemed like such a gift; the mess and the chaos seemed less relevant. It's not that keeping her house clean was no longer important—it was just that it was no longer an emergency!

I hope you enjoy the stories in this book as much as I have. I believe they will inspire you and enrich your life in positive ways. I'm sure your life is filled with rich and insightful stories. Perhaps, in reading these, you'll find yourself remembering a few of your own.

Treasure the gift of life,
Richard Carlson
Benicia, California
March 2002

THE DON'T SWEAT
STORIES

PART I

DON'T SWEAT THE SMALL STUFF IN EVERYDAY LIFE

All Is Calm

Christmas at my house used to be like this—decorate the house, wrap the presents, send the cards, bake the cookies, and on and on with a million things to do. We'd sing "Joy to the World" and "Deck the Halls," but wonder what happened to "Silent Night," holy night, and all is calm. It sure wasn't calm in my place, which was always the location of our extended family's annual Christmas Eve gathering.

I had the most and youngest children (seven children in thirteen years, four of whom were born sixteen months apart). I also had the most room and was best equipped to handle the needs that went with the various ages of my children—toys, places to sleep, diaper-changing location, walkers, and the like. Besides that, my relatives didn't really want to have to deal with all my kids at their house. I understood and didn't mind, honest. I loved having the whole family over on Christmas Eve.

What I didn't love were all the preparations. When all the gifts were finally bought and wrapped, the cards addressed by hand, stamped, and sent, hundreds of tiny outside lights in place, and the tree decorated with all of our treasured ornaments, it was time for the annual cookie baking ritual. That meant hours and hours of lost cleaning time spent peeking into the oven to see if the cookies were done yet while yelling at my children, "Don't get the flour all over the place. Stop eating the chocolate chips or we won't have enough, and please stop fighting over who gets to lick the bowl. We're making a ton of cookies; you'll all get a bowl." Cookie making was hardly a Norman Rockwell activity for me.

Next we had to tackle the house, which rarely looked anything like the pictures in *House Beautiful*. Most of the time it looked as if it had just been ransacked by some not-too-bright burglars, looking for money and jewelry. They'd have to be extremely dim-witted to think we had anything of value besides a front room full of Little Tykes child-sized furniture. Most of the time I put up with a very lived-in house. The annual Christmas Eve family gathering was one of the few days I demanded Martha Stewart–type perfection and hospital cleanliness.

If I wanted the house magazine-perfect, though, it was all up to me. The children helped as little as they could get away with, while I sweated over the smallest stuff you can imagine: I organized cabinets no one would look in, changed sheets no one would see, washed floors that would be dirty five minutes after the company arrived, and cleaned the oven, stove burners, and grates, even though no one was going to care whether they were clean or not as long as the food was good. Then there was the food. I had to cook, but not just normal things: I had to make special stuff, Christmas tradition stuff.

Cheesecake, pumpkin pie, lasagna, Jell-O molds, Italian beef, and ham. Then there was the bean casserole only Aunt Ruth liked, but still, it had to be made. It was tradition. Finally, I had to wash the "good dishes" that we used only on Christmas Eve, leaving them wrapped and stashed away from tiny hands the rest of the year.

Was I frazzled? You bet. Preparing for our family's Christmas gathering was a tense, rushed, extremely stressful time for me. Even during the last minutes before the company came I was rushing around finishing the last-minute jobs of cleaning the bathrooms and mopping the kitchen floor, which I usually did after the whole family and I were dressed and ready for our company. Remember, in my house things wouldn't stay clean any longer than five minutes.

How did I finally break these hectic, stressful Christmas traditions? I didn't. The weather did it for me.

It had been a very cold winter in Chicago the year I discovered what Christmas Eve should be like. On that Christmas Eve, the weather forecasters were predicting the temperature would drop to twenty-five degrees below zero. My company was to begin arriving at six P.M. I was frantically doing all the last-minute things when the phone rang. It was my father. He and my mother were not coming. It was too cold. "What if we have car trouble? We could be in real trouble. We're sorry but..."

Two down, I thought, but continued cleaning the floor and telling the younger kids to put away their toys so the house would look nice when the rest of the company came. But the phone began to ring again and again, like the tinkly refrain in a peppy Christmas tune. One by one relatives all called with the same reasons for not coming.

By five-thirty, I knew no one was coming. I stopped cleaning. I took off my good dress and put on my comfortable jeans. We got out the Monopoly game, and with two of my older children's friends, we played Monopoly. We opened potato chips, ate all the appetizers I had made. The younger children got out all the toys they had put away and spread them all over the floor. We laughed; we played cards; we ate a delicious dinner on undecorated plain white paper plates. We even sang Christmas carols.

Since that year, I've simplified our family's Christmas gathering. I don't deep-clean the house before the company comes; I just straighten. I don't make a lot of fancy food. I make one or two things I enjoy making, and so do other family members. The kids and I make only one kind of cookie—chocolate chip. Sometimes we run out of chips because we eat them all, but that's okay. The cookies rarely make it to Christmas Eve anyway. We don't use my fancy Christmas dishes; we eat off poinsettia-and-holly-decorated paper plates so the women don't have to spend the rest of the evening cleaning up. Instead we laugh, reminisce, and play games and cards.

Sometimes we sing Christmas carols, including "Silent Night." My house, full of my large, loving family, certainly isn't silent, but now when I sing the line *all is calm, all is bright,* I truly mean it.

— *Carol Kloskowski*

The awkwardness of being strangers was gone, and my nervousness had melted away. Since they both felt everything at church was going "fine," we spent almost all our time—a couple of hours visit—talking about life in general until my new "old friends" walked me to the door and bade me a hearty good night. And to think this was a task I'd dreaded.

"Thank you for everything, Mr. and Mrs. Johnson," I replied. "I had such a wonderful time!"

Still standing in the doorway, their expressions changed slowly from smiles to mild confusion. "Mr. and Mrs. Johnson?" they said simultaneously. "We're the Hanovers. Mr. and Mrs. Johnson live down the road at 1887. Our address is 1881."

We three stood there speechless, no one quite knowing what to say from this point. And since none of us did figure anything out, we all just burst out laughing—a hearty, bent-over-at-the-waist, cheeks-aching hysteria. What had just happened here? For the past two hours I'd been sitting at the wrong house talking about a church they assumed was their own—St. Lucas Lutheran—but was in fact my own, Peace United.

Driving home and still laughing, I felt great. Really great! So I made two last stops: the first at the Johnsons', to make another church call, and the last one at the grocery store. There was a magazine I needed to buy, and an article I wanted to finish reading.

— *Rochelle Pennington*

23

The Honeypot

As a speaker, I have been in many different places and have been privileged to meet many people. Many are in fairly ordinary situations, hardworking folks who've been asked by their companies to meet for the day in an ordinary hotel conference room, clutching cups of watery coffee and trying to stay focused on what I am saying. I'm accustomed to the routine, accustomed to the travel, and accustomed to having most of my speeches go smoothly. Not always, though…

I was scheduled to speak in Akiachuk, Alaska, to a group of Alaskan villagers on the topic of communication and customer service. Alaska isn't that easy to get to, and this part of Alaska was pretty remote. To get there, I flew from Vancouver to Seattle, Seattle to Anchorage, Anchorage to Bethel. The plan was to stay at a bed-and-breakfast in Bethel and then fly by Cessna to Akiachuk the following morning to do the seminar. It seemed like something I could handle, so I readily agreed.

When I arrived in Bethel, there was a change in plans. A big change, actually. I would be taking a boat, spending the night in Akiachuk, and then flying back by Cessna to Bethel after the seminar. Now when I say *boat*, I don't mean a large passenger ship. This was a six-foot aluminum dinghy with an outboard motor. It took us two hours of crossing open water to get to the village. I huddled deep inside my warm coat the whole time.

At last we found the village, but I realized I didn't know where I would be staying. No cute bed-and-breakfasts in this town. The CEO who hired me said I would be staying at his place. He asked me what I wanted for dinner, and I said fish. He grinned. "Great, we'll catch our dinner later."

His house had no plumbing. As tactfully as possible, he tried to explain the "honeypot" in my room. For those of you who don't have older relatives telling you stories of life before toilets, let's just say it was a chamber pot. This business trip was not turning out quite as I'd expected.

I kept mentally reminding myself to stay calm, to focus on the positive. We went fishing for our dinner and were covered in blackflies and mosquitoes. I didn't catch any fish, and by this time it was ten at night on an August evening—in Alaska, it doesn't get dark until midnight. On the ride back to the village he ran out of gas. Once that was fixed, we stopped at a fish camp so that I could see what one looked like. When we returned to the boat, it was full of water. By now it was almost midnight.

We finally had dinner. I went to sleep, got up the next morning, and couldn't shower. No plumbing, remember? I fixed myself the best I could and went to do the seminar.

My talk did not get off to a stellar start. From the looks on the faces of the folks sitting before me, I could tell I was bombing. During a break, the CEO came to me and asked me to set up a role-playing exercise, thinking that it might help the mood. I wasn't sure it would, but I did it anyway. All hell broke loose in the room as long-suppressed emotions between coworkers came to the surface. It was a total disaster—chairs flying, tables turned over, everyone yelling at each other.

At that point I took a deep breath and decided to try a different approach. I asked everyone to form a circle with their chairs. I used a pen as a talking stick and we threw the workbooks away. For the next two hours we focused on making sure each person was heard.

After that dreadful start, the seminar did turn out to be a success after all, and I flew as planned by Cessna back to Bethel. My flight home was the following morning.

Shortly after takeoff, there was an announcement that we would be turning and making an emergency landing back in Bethel. Once we were back in the Bethel airport, I broke down in tears. A sympathetic woman came up to me, put her arm around me, and listened patiently as I poured it all out.

I finished sobbing out my tale and looked up at her, expecting to see a look of sympathy. Instead, she was smiling and shaking her head. "What a wonderful experience you had! You had to take a small boat to Akiachuk—what an adventure! Yes, you had to use a honeypot—but your host had to empty it! Yes, you had to fish for your dinner, but he cooked it! Yes, you ran out of gas and got stuck on the riverbank, but you got to see an Alaskan fish camp! Yes, your plane had to turn around and you won't be home today, but you are alive! Yes, the group did not follow the regular rules of conduct, but you followed your intuition and you were successful! What a blessing you have received."

I listened in disbelief. Was she right? Had I been lucky every step of the way, lucky enough to have experienced new and varied things? Yes! And with that, I realized that she was absolutely right. I'd had an experience few others would ever have. What luck! I was in the right place at the right time to learn and to help others.

—*Cheryl Cran*

911 Hugs

"**D**id you hear?" Troy, one of my coworkers, brushed past me and snatched up the phone on the desk in front of mine. "Hear what?" I asked him, tensing up just a little when I saw the look of concern on his face. My first thought was that he had heard a storm was on its way. Maybe a tornado warning was out. Troy finished dialing, and then, while waiting for his wife to answer the phone, he told me, "A plane just crashed into the World Trade Center." Thus the morning began. As it dragged on mercilessly, I began to wonder if it was ever going to end. Throughout the day, we employees were drawn over and over again to the break room and the television there, then back to our individual departments to tend to our responsibilities. Thankfully, and understandably, there were very few customers at the home design store. It felt strange to me that we were all still working. We put one foot in front of the other; we were able to function, or at least to go through the motions. Amazing. It seemed strange, too, that some were shopping.

Once I came out of the break room to see a customer looking through a wallpaper book, and wondered how that was possible, in light of what was going on. Reminded that I had a job to do, I approached her and asked if there was anything I could help her with. When she looked up from the brightly colored pages, I could tell she had been crying. Her response was, "I came here to get away from the TV." I understood. We talked like friends. There was no mention of weather or prices or wallpaper. We actually shared a few minutes of meaningful discussion about the compassion we felt for those in the area of the attacks, their and our loved ones, life, God. It was not your average customer/salesperson exchange. It was not your average day of average interests, or of average trivialities.

Later, a customer stood at the counter looking at samples of mini-blinds. I had just spent another couple of minutes in the break room, where several of us clustered together staring at the TV screen. Tears ran down my cheeks, but it didn't matter. No one noticed. We weren't looking at each other. The TV had our full attention. Exiting the break room, I walked over to the customer and asked her how she was doing today, just as if it were a regular Tuesday. She told me she had felt she needed to get out for a while and thought this was a good place to go. She smiled and I smiled back. But then, because I had to tell someone, I said, "People are jumping out of windows," just as if that too was a normal thing to say. Our eyes locked and held. This could not be real. We talked; we had to.

I tried to help another customer choose blinds for several windows. I showed her various samples and together we looked through them. We discussed options periodically, but were finding it increasingly difficult to stay off the subject of all we had been seeing and hearing on television. It soon became evident that our hearts were not totally in this particular activity. It also became obvious that I could not concentrate on the simplest math, as she and I compared prices. "I'm sorry," I told her. "I can't concentrate. It is hard to work today." This middle-aged customer, a stranger, looked at me, and her eyes instantly filled with tears. As if surprised by her own thought, she said, "Then let's hug!" There we stood in the middle of the decorating design department, two women who had never seen each other before that day, locked in a full-fledged bear hug. During the unforgettably devastating circumstances of that particular day, I would never have dreamed that a hug could contain so much comfort. It was a couple of days later that I heard President Bush say something that went straight to my heart and reminded me of that moment. He said we should "share our grief and draw strength from one another." How amazing that one way to do that is a simple hug. Give hugs. God bless.

—*Alison Peters*

Time Isn't Money

I learned to stop sweating the small stuff when I truly accepted my mortality. From that point on, I had no time for the small stuff.

A simple example was the time our hotel room was robbed. Leaving my hotel room, I passed a stranger in the hallway. After I'd gone, he entered with a key and cleaned out the contents.

Every morning for the next few weeks I woke up with the same thought. I was mad as hell, wishing I could be back in that hallway confronting the thief. It finally dawned on me that he was *still* stealing from me. First he had taken my possessions; now he was taking my precious time and using it in an unhealthy way.

I suddenly had a vision of this thief pawning our things and using the money to buy Christmas presents for his children. I found myself smiling at the thought and thinking I should have thrown in another hundred dollars or so in order to really make his kids happy. From then on, the thought of this thief brought me smiles, not resentment.

So later when our son's garage was robbed, it was easy to offer him comfort. I told him that the thief hadn't bought his mother a birthday present in ten years. With the money from the burglary, however, he could finally buy her a gift, apologize for the past, and share his love. My son smiled at his crazy father's theories. But I got him to smile, didn't I? And he smiles every time the robbery is mentioned.

Accept the fact that you are here for a limited time and decide not to let the small stuff take your time. Because time isn't money—it is everything. You can then spend your time on the things and the people that you love.

—*Bernie Siegel*

Rainy-Day Sunshine

Both of my parents died young from cancer. As a result, I have always done my best to support the American Cancer Society and other similar organizations. Now with my fortieth birthday looming near, I have become painfully aware of my mortality. As a result, I have recently made major changes in my life, adopting a new slogan of "life's too short." I decided to dedicate my time to fund-raising and helping as many charitable causes as I could.

Recently I spent a large part of the day on the phone. I first spoke with a neighbor suffering from cancer, then with another neighbor undergoing treatment for leukemia, and then with three different friends who have each recently lost a parent. I also spent several hours on the phone looking for local businesses willing to donate the canisters I needed to help me begin my collection efforts for my most recent fund-raising undertaking. All this was to no avail. Phone call after phone call was a disappointment, so I decided it was time to just go buy them myself.

As I went from store to store, the skies gradually darkened. As I was leaving one store, the skies opened up with raindrops the size of quarters and a heavy downpour. Unhappy shoppers huddled by the entrance. Some were lucky enough to have hoods or umbrellas; some were opting to wait it out. But all were grumbling, annoyed at this change in the weather. It was quite clear to me that these people were intent on letting a rainstorm ruin their day. Not me—I was on a mission. I had canisters to find and a project to begin, and I was quite confident that a little rain would not hurt me.

I made my way past the people and out toward my next destination. As I walked through the parking lot getting totally drenched, I glanced up at the sky and smiled, thanking God for the ability to shop on my own, drive myself, and walk in the rain. I thought about the people I'd spoken to that day and what they were all facing or enduring. I thought about my neighbor who can't sit outside because of the damage that could result from the chemicals on the lawn, or the sun could cause to her skin. I thought about what others would give for the chance to move as freely as I could at that moment. Why sweat the small stuff, indeed.

As I crossed the parking lot, a police officer standing under the store's awning shouted: "Hey, you better run, you don't wanna get wet, do you?" Still smiling, I looked over my shoulder at him and called back, "If getting wet is the worst thing that happens to me today, then I'll consider myself pretty fortunate!"

—*Becky Paumier*

34

Always a Nice Day

Each year I take a trip to San Antonio, Texas, for the annual convention of the Texas Music Educators Association. One of the highlights of this event is always the concert given by the Texas All-State Symphony Orchestra, made up of some of the finest high school musicians in the country. This year was no exception. The orchestra performed this night with the skill and finesse common to a professional orchestra, but there was something far more special in the air. Orchestra and conductor seemed like one being.

As an encore, the group performed the *Nimrod* variation of Sir Edward Elgar's *Enigma Variations*, following an emotional and eloquent introduction by the conductor, in which he explained the piece's theme of eternal friendship. He closed his oration by giving thanks to the young musicians and sharing a custom from his childhood in England. He stated that whenever one encounters a special moment, one need only press his thumb and fourth finger together and the moment will be cast in memory forever.

Inspired, I floated out of the auditorium. Arriving at my hotel room, I realized I had yet to have dinner, although it was quite late. I picked up the phone and ordered a pizza from an establishment I'd noticed earlier in the day. I figured a nighttime stroll to pick up my dinner would afford me the opportunity to bask in the memory of the evening's concert.

I arrived at the restaurant and gave the cashier my name. As I waited for my pizza in silence, she began complaining about her work schedule and expressing relief that the next day was her day off. She then remarked that it was certain to rain; after all, it *was* her day off. Still basking in the glow of Elgar's embers, I felt optimism sweep through me.

"It might not rain," I told her. "Does the forecast call for rain?"

"I don't know," she answered. "I just know that I'm planning to go to the park with some friends, so it's sure to rain."

"Well, maybe it won't." I don't quite know why, but I was stubborn in my insistence. She squinted slightly. Who was the nutty stranger insisting that the weather would hold?

"It's just that every time I plan to go to the park it always rains, so I know it will tomorrow." Tilting her head defiantly, she raised her eyebrows as if daring me to disagree again.

"Well, I'll bet tomorrow will be different. Besides, even if it rains, you will still be with your friends." I wouldn't allow her to be negative.

She flashed me a half smile as if to concede, giving up her pessimism. About this time my pizza arrived. She rang it up, took my money, and thanked me in just the manner she had been trained.

As I took my pizza and started to leave, she said, "This is when I'm supposed to say 'have a nice night,' but somehow I know *you will*."

I just smiled. I left the establishment and crossed the street, balancing my precious pizza. I had to carry my pizza in one hand, you see; the other was occupied. My thumb and fourth finger were firmly engaged.

—*Paul Stephens*

Celebration of Life

On my way home from coaching basketball yesterday, I was listening to WGN, my favorite talk radio station out of Chicago. I could tell right away that there was something wrong by the somber mood of the speaker. There had been a plane crash. Two small planes collided into each other over a northern suburb of Chicago. What made the story hit close to home was that Bob Collins, the morning show man for WGN, had been the pilot of one of the planes and was killed.

Later that night, as I made my forty-minute drive to my third-shift job, I listened as the commentators reminisced about and paid tribute to a man who was loved by many. They told story after story, describing him as the ultimate friend and a man who had lived life to the fullest. Genuine love and affection poured in from radio listeners all over the country. The more I listened to how this man had influenced those around him, the more discouraged I became.

Why? you ask. I was discouraged because I wanted to know why we wait until somebody has passed away before we tell her how much we love her. Why do we wait until someone can't hear us before we let him know how much he meant to us? Why do we wait until it is too late before we recall the good qualities of a person? Why do we build people up after they have gone into eternity? What good does it do then?

We share memory after memory as we laugh, cry, and think back about what was positive in a person's life. Yes, it does help us cope with the grief of losing someone special to us, and, yes, it does bring those who are coping with the loss closer together. Unfortunately, as we lovingly remember this person, our words fall short of the ears that most needed to hear them.

Just once I would like to see a celebration of life instead of a gathering of death. A celebration in which stories are told, eyes mist over, laughter rings out, and as the speaker concludes his or her loving tribute, the person so honored rises from his or her chair and hugs the speaker. Wouldn't that be something! The special people get to hear the stories and come to the realization that they have made a difference on this earth, and all this is done well before they leave their earthly bodies and go into eternity.

When the inevitable funerals finally come, we can say good-bye with the knowledge that these people knew exactly how those around them felt about them while they were here on earth.

I now have a stronger resolve to tell those around me how much they mean to me. I am going to let my wife know just how loved and appreciated she is, not only by my words but also by my actions. I am going to play Batman with my four-year-old more often, and in the middle of our fun, I am going to grab him, hug him tightly, and tell him how thankful I am that he is my son. I am going to sneak into my sleeping toddler's bedroom, kiss his chubby cheek, and thank God for the bundle of joy He has brought into my life. Each day I will make a point to tell both of my boys how much I love them, whether they are four or eighteen! I am going to let family and friends know the tremendous impact they have had on my life.

Finally, I am going to let the high school players I coach know that I look forward to each and every minute that I get to spend with them in the gym.

Do you love someone? Then tell them! Has someone had an influence in your life? Then give them a call! Has someone made a difference in your life? Then write them a letter or send them an e-mail! Don't let another day go by without letting that person know. There is something special about a letter that expresses feelings of love toward another. I don't know about you, but I have letters and cards from people that I have saved for years, and from time to time I get them out and reread them. They can turn a depressing day into one in which I realize just how blessed and lucky I am.

Life is too short to leave kind words unsaid. The words you say or the letter you write might just make all the difference in the world.

—Michael T. Powers

The License Plate Renewal

Face it: There are some things in life that most of us do not care about. The fact that the decal on my car's license plate had expired a year and two months ago was not a life-threatening disaster. Nevertheless, I, as someone who always took pride in keeping car-related bureaucratic necessities up-to-date, saw this as a major failure. Why didn't I look at my plates more often? Why didn't I receive a notice after I moved?

I *thought* I had reported the change of address to the Department of Motor Vehicles. Since none of these explanations or hindsight remedies would get me a new, shiny decal on my license plate, I decided to face the inevitable penalties, shame, and additional late fees, which I preferred not to call delinquent fees.

I drove to the local Department of Motor Vehicles branch with extreme care, being watchful for cars with lights on their roofs. Luckily, I escaped all manner of official vehicle. Even if they caught me in the DMV parking lot, it would be obvious I was trying hard to comply with the law. Here I was, right at the kingdom's door to beg for mercy. Surely I would be given a reprieve by the higher powers of the road since I was turning myself in.

I entered and looked around, shifty-eyed. I spotted the renewals window and shuffled to it, clutching at my outdated registration. Facing the stern man behind the counter, I humbly told him my tale of woe. I was in second grade again and waiting in line to be punished by the teacher for not turning in homework that I didn't know was due. As he struggled to hear my soft voice, which included my license plate number, he typed the information into his instrument of evil, grabbed a new decal from a drawer, and informed me that I owed the same amount I would normally pay if I had paid on time. This covered the period I should have paid for plus the remainder of the two years. He waited calmly in silence for me to pay.

I stared blankly at him for so long that he had to repeat the amount. I insisted on asking him if there was a late fee or penalty. He shook his head and smiled. As I walked out of the building and stuck the decal to my license plate, I realized all I had done was raise my blood pressure. Although I do not recommend ignoring such legal matters, nothing happened. No ticket, no penalty, no reprimand, no embarrassment, no handcuffs—no sweat. It was so much smaller than I thought. So much smaller... Even smaller than the beads of sweat on my forehead.

—*Joe Sainz*

Looking Up

It is time I started looking up, the way I did when I was a kid. I have been so busy doing unto others and not to myself, so consumed with marching to the beat of a martyr and not missing a step, so absorbed in the pity party where women my age like to gather, that I forgot what every child instinctively knows: A neck is made to swivel for a reason, and if you don't use it, you'll lose out on what can happen when earth meets the sky.

The parting of clouds should be reason enough to make me look up and enjoy. Evening sky in the Northwest in March is not usually as smooth and streaked with color as it was the other night, but I usually don't mess with the sky. Even when cloud pillows wrapped in pastel cases float overhead, I seldom look up. If that had been all there was in the sky that evening—just the parting of the clouds—I would have missed it.

The coming forth of stars should be reason enough to make me look up and enjoy. I once wondered how stars move around in the sky but somehow stay connected. When I remember to look up, I can still spot Orion, ready to shoot, and the Seven Sisters huddled together and the two dippers hanging on their celestial pegs. But most of the time I forget to look up. If that had been all there was in the sky that evening—just the parting of clouds and the twinkling of stars—I would have missed it.

The presence of the moon should be reason enough to make me look up and enjoy, especially when it is as full as a sunflower in September. But when you've seen a full moon once, you've seen them all, that's what I figured: a sideways glance through the car window or as I take out the garbage or fumble for my house keys has been plenty of moon for me. If that had been all there was in the sky that evening—just the parting of clouds and the twinkling of stars and the big round yellow moon—I would have missed it.

The sight of a shadow nibbling away at the moon should be reason enough to make me look up and enjoy. Yet when an eclipse comes along, I might glance out the window a time or two, but there is no need, I figured, for me to crane my neck for hours the way people did in times gone by. They didn't know an eclipse of the moon is merely our earth throwing its shadow around, just as I used to do when I was a kid, making huge shadowy rabbit heads with floppy ears on the dining room wall with my fingers. If that had been all there was in the sky that evening—just the parting of clouds and the twinkling of stars and the crumbling away of the big round yellow moon—I would have missed it.

The vision of a visitor among the stars should be reason enough to make me look up and enjoy. But the night was cold, the wind kicked up, and a glimpse of a comet out my front window was all I had time and energy for. I didn't even take my binoculars out of the drawer. If that had been all there was in the sky that evening—first the parting of clouds and next the twinkling of stars and then the big round yellow moon turning black and finally the sight of a comet passing by—I would have missed it.

But everything came at once and the voices of children finally drew me outside. I saw clouds pulled aside like curtains drawn for a play. From my backyard, I watched the moon shrink. The darker the sky became, the bigger the stars looked. As I moved to the front yard, I could see a comet streak across the sky.

It was so much more exciting than usual, I didn't know how to act. I paced from front yard to back until the moon finally rose high enough. I could stand in one place and see the whole thing: a comet with a forked tail streaking over a star-cluttered sky, while a black rubber-stamped moon looked on. And to think, I almost missed the whole thing.

No wonder I am starting to look up the way I did when I was a kid, and down to watch ants and toward sunsets dripping over mountains like syrup on ice cream. Nothing I have to do for the rest of my life is more important than this.

—*Gloria MacKay*

Stop and Smell the Cinnamon

I've spent much of my life racing up and down the West Coast from California to Washington. My family lives in Northern California, but has an old family farm in Washington's Skagit Valley, where we spend summers and holidays. The six or seven hundred miles between Northern California and the Skagit Valley are filled with variety: the quaint little towns in Oregon, the used bookstores in Portland, the museums in Seattle. At least, I've heard they are filled with variety. I wouldn't know, actually, because we've always been in too much of a rush to stop and take a look.

When I was a child, my father set the frantic pace. Up early and out on the road in an ever-changing series of station wagons. A quick sandwich near the Oregon border. A restless night in the same motel every time—the Village Green in Cottage Grove. Frequent looks at the watch on his wrist and the same admonition every trip: "Hurry up, we're making good time."

Making good time was the point, you see, not exploring the towns we were whizzing through. I'd look longingly out the window for mile after mile, thinking, "When I grow up, I'm going to stop in

46

every single one of these places and see what's there."

But when I did grow up and begin to make the same drive myself, I felt just as rushed. In my early twenties, I brought a friend along on a springtime trip up to the farm. As we rocketed past Ashland, Oregon, that morning, I waved my hand out the window and said, "This is a really cute little town, I think. We ought to stop here some time..." We didn't.

And now I make that same drive several times a year with my husband and our two boys. "Come on, let's go," my husband, Peter, calls out as he herds us toward the car to begin the two-day journey up Interstate 5. "I want to make good time." I watch out the window as the same small towns flash by. Driving through California we pass Maxwell, Orland, Redding, Weed, and Yreka. In Oregon we whiz by Ashland, Grants Pass, Roseburg, Wolf Creek, and Salem. Once we are in Washington the countdown begins. We're pretty close to the farm, but not there yet...First we must drive through Vancouver, Olympia, all of Seattle, Everett, and Stanwood. Only when we see the turnoff for La Conner, the tiny town up the road from Beaver Marsh Farm, do we breathe a sigh of relief and relax, knowing that our vacation is about to begin.

I thought about those towns this past Christmas as we roared past in our old Ford Explorer. This was a new thing, going up during December instead of spring, summer, or fall. "Wonder what Mt. Shasta City looks like with Christmas lights," I thought as I saw the freeway exit sign go by. "Or maybe Dunsmuir. Must be kind of cute, an old downtown area draped with twinkling lights. On the way back we should stop and check it out." And we drove on.

It was my turn to drive as we passed through southern Oregon. This time of year the sun sets a little after five in the afternoon, but despite the early hour, both boys and Peter had nodded off in the darkness. We went past the green Oregon exit signs, one after the other. I steered the Ford past a sign for Quines Creek, reminding drivers that it was just a few miles ahead. Another sign reminded drivers that there was food and gas at this exit, and that the restaurant was called Heaven on Earth. Heaven on Earth? I smiled at the size of their claim. I'd read mentions in food magazines of this little place, how they serve the best cinnamon rolls in the Western United States. *Someday I'll stop there*, I'd thought as I read the review. Someday? I glanced at my watch. We were making pretty good time, but still...a big warm cinnamon roll, just out of the oven? *This is it*, I decided. *I'm stopping! I'm going to buy myself a cinnamon bun right here, right now, travel schedule be damned.*

My husband woke up as I slowed down and signaled at the end of the exit. "What's going on?" he asked, blurry from his unexpected nap. "Do we need gas?" "No," I replied. He looked at me, puzzled. "Oh, are you tired of driving? Do you want to switch drivers?" "No," I said again. "I'm going to stop and buy one of these cinnamon rolls." He looked at his watch. "Now? You're going to stop now? But we're making such good time..."

"Yes! I'm going to stop. I'm tired of not stopping. It's time to take a look around in Oregon instead of just driving straight through. I've waited forty years to pull off this freeway. I'm going to stop and buy myself a cinnamon roll and a cup of coffee."

The car rolled to a stop at the side of the log-cabin-style restaurant. Tiny white Christmas lights strung along the edge of the building cast a soft glow inside the car on our boys, still asleep in their car seats. "I'll stay here," my husband whispered. "You go inside."

I pulled open the heavy wooden door. The smell was heavenly —warm and yeasty, sweet and sugary. I stepped inside and breathed deeply. What was the big hurry? Why were we sweating the small stuff over this? If we got to Washington half an hour later, did it really matter?

The waitress placed a towering cinnamon bun dripping with glaze before me. No, it didn't matter at all, I realized as I savored the first bite. And maybe, just maybe, I'd stop here again on the way back through.

—*Jennifer Basye Sander*

A Christmas Pageant
to Remember

It *was* my signature. There was no denying it. Not that I intended to, it was just that I wanted to make sure that I had really signed up on the sheet posted in the church hallway recruiting mothers to volunteer their help at the children's Christmas pageant practice. If I hadn't, I could have sneaked out of that very pageant practice and headed back home. But there was my name in blue ink.

It was only ten-thirty in the morning, and these little cherubs had gotten the best of me. Merry Christmas, ho, ho, ho.

Three of the shepherds were sword fighting with their staffs in the back of the sanctuary. One little gal, a first-year music student, was pounding out some rendition of "Away in a Manger" on the piano (so she said—but oh, my head), and someone had sat on top of the Hershey kisses I intended to pass out as rewards. Now they were melted into the beautiful red upholstery in pew 4. What next?

Maggie. Now Maggie's intentions were noble enough. She really *did* want to help. And so she kept all of us mothers abreast on who was doing what bad stuff and when. It was a minute-by-minute report of who stuck gum under what chair, who made a naughty face at one of the teachers when she wasn't looking, and who had put a diaper on the Baby Jesus doll without asking first. Yes, in her little "fingernails on chalkboard" voice, warden Maggie tried to help, bless her soul. (As if we didn't have our hands full enough keeping track of what we ourselves caught these little buggers doing.)

I couldn't help but wonder how in the world this pageant was going to get pulled together by Christmas Eve. But then the big night arrived, and it did.

Was it perfect? No. But was it precious? Absolutely. Even the glitches. It seemed the same young miss who insisted the Baby Lord be in clean underwear also insisted He be warm. And so she brought along one of her brother's Green Bay Packers hats from home. It didn't matter to her that we were inside the church, and it was plenty warm in there for a Jesus doll. What mattered to her was that we were *pretending* we were outside where it was cold. Details, details.

So the Holy Family—Mary, Joseph, and Jesus in a Packers hat —took their places that year beside the altar, while our young maestro played her out-of-tune version of "Away in a Manger" while smiling from ear to ear on the bench. And we smiled back.

—*Rochelle M. Pennington*

Praise

The events of the day swirled in my brain. Stress's heavy presence loomed like the suffocating air outside. A screaming, crimson-faced infant thrashed in my arms. Arching her back furiously, my tiny daughter Katelyn screamed her discontent in a high-pitched cry that echoed in my ears. She was suddenly too hungry to allow the thirty seconds it would require to get into feeding position to pass without a fight.

Sleep had evaded me for the nine weeks of her life, and my spirits were frazzled. All that day, clammy Midwestern humidity stuck to me like a wool coat. This muggy Wednesday brought us sweltering gray skies for the tenth day in a row. Rain pelted me as I struggled, diaper bag and baby carrier in tow, from my husband Nicholas's car to the house. I had just returned from an exasperating trip to the bank. Seems the automatic deposit of Nic's paycheck was not so automatic after all, and we had bounced sixteen checks in its wake.

The day was rounded off nicely by a visit from Nic's children from an earlier marriage, something I diligently tried to adjust to. Their father and I had initially been involved in a long-distance relationship, so I had not been around his kids very often, though I had known them for years. One week before our baby's birth I found myself in a new town and a new house with a new husband and three stepchildren; their mom lived nearby. Twenty-five hundred miles away, my family and familiar surroundings carried on without me. My new small town boasted one grocery store, and everyone knew my husband. "Are you the new wife or the old one?" people inquired when they saw my new last name on a check stub at a local store.

The baby in my arms screamed with renewed zest. Too mad to eat, she twisted her body and threw her arms up in utter dismay. Overwhelmed, I found myself without the ability to produce positive thoughts. A pounding headache overwhelmed me. The baby kept crying, the black sky kept producing rain, and my head kept pulsating.

Trying to decide if I should cry or scream to express how much I hated my life at that precise moment, out of the blue I remembered someone on television encouraging viewers to snap themselves out of negative responses by praising not only the positive but everything in sight. This act supposedly would turn the world around. It sounded like a bunch of hooey, but I leaped up and handed my infant to her father when he attempted to pass through the room before disappearing again.

As I sprinted for the door, through its leaded glass window I could see that the rain had let up, at least temporarily. *Praise that*, I huffed to myself.

I stomped down the long, cement driveway toward the road. *Praise Indiana streets.* The humidity mercifully let up temporarily because of the rain. *Praise less humidity and almost breathable air.* I passed brick and stone monuments that housed cast-iron mailboxes at the end of long brick driveways leading to homes with matching brick and stone. *Praise mailboxes, the letters they hold and the people who send them.* "Built in 1906," a lopsided sign as old as its inscription boasted, announcing the age of the residence. *Praise 1906 and the homes built then.* Walking into a cloud of mosquitoes that hovered in a ball, I cursed the creatures. Oops. *Praise mosquitoes...* Hmmm, I had to think fast...*for they feed small birds.*

Each home I passed was enveloped by a grove of trees. Some houses were designed by famous architects and considered experimental for the times. Others were quite traditional, built for well-to-do businessmen near the turn of the century. Even by today's standards, they were massive estates. It was like stepping back into a period of opulence and wealth. *Praise beautiful things that last for centuries!* All stood on well-groomed one- or two-acre lots. *Praise spacious and expansive grounds! Praise that we could rent here for a year while the homeowner was temporarily out of the state. Praise this brief visit to this lavish place we otherwise would have missed.*

To my left, leaves from abundant trees covered rooftops. *Praise trees.* I had never noticed that there were so many. There were hundreds, no, thousands of them, towering as high as three- and four-story buildings. *Praise tall timbers!* Branches from trees planted across the street from each other extended over the road and entwined, creating a massive canopy of many shades of green. *Praise green leaves and twisted branches that embrace over the road! Praise the shade they create on hot summer days!* Up the street at the intersection of two narrow roads, the trees were so profuse they arched into what appeared to be a wooded tunnel. The street below was barely wet due to nature's massive umbrella. *Praise!* Ahead, the moon glowed like a faded cotton ball. Dimmed by the humid air, it was a fuzzy orb beyond the treetops. *Praise the gentle radiance of the moon on a humid night!*

I passed two-story brick homes with wraparound porches whose porch swings invited friends and neighbors to stop by during spring walks. *Praise porches! Praise neighbors! Praise this neighborhood!* Pointed rooftops housed attics that perhaps contained generations of family treasures and all the out-of-season clothing. *Praise attics! Praise Great-Grandma's cotillion dress!* Basement lights illuminated the bottom windows of some structures. *Praise basements, for in them you can store everything!* Our basement had the contents of my former home in boxes, plus a washer and a dryer. It even had a coal room with plenty of coal still in the bin next to a massive furnace that heated the two stories above it. The home had been heated with coal until the present owner put in central heat and air. Years before, his grandmother and then mother would rise before dawn on bitter cold mornings and shovel the coal to get it burning before the rest of the family stirred. *Praise being born in modern times. Praise central heat and air and automatic washers and dryers! Praise! Praise! Praise! Praise diaper services. Praise disposable diapers on long trips. Praise having choices! Praise public toilets and running water!*

Many secrets about the hidden beauty of my new neighborhood were revealed during this praise walk of mine. Actually, everything I praised was neither secret nor hidden. It had been right in front of me for over ten weeks. I had not noticed the splendor of these surroundings because I had stopped looking beyond myself months ago and felt only the stresses of my new life, not noticing the beauty in it. *Praise PRAISE WALKS!* Renewed, I was ready to take on my life again. I breathed in the thick air and praised the person who suggested praising all things, good and bad. *Praise wisdom and good advice! Praise taking good advice. Praise the kindness of strangers!*

Circling back, I headed up the narrow drive that led to our aged house. Pushing the heavy front door open, I heard the baby's howls.

"Where have you *been?* You have been gone for thirty minutes!" My husband, his face now as red as the child's, held out the wailing baby. "It's *your* turn again!"

Praise healthy babies. Praise the couch. Praise the ceiling. Praise the television set. Praise ironing boards and electricity. Praise electric can openers. . . .

—*Suzan Davis*

Visiting Henry

He was visibly relaxed, using his heels to rock the porch swing back and forth. Observing the antics of squirrels in a cluster of pecan trees. Gauging the weather through squinted eyes. Watching time stroll by. My husband Stephen had been on the job a few days now, watching his customer. It was the same thing every day. The man sat on a double swing suspended from the ceiling of the back porch, and the only breaks he took were for lunch and calls of nature. He was in his late eighties, and I'll just call him Henry Foster. A slight man in coveralls with soft blue eyes and wispy hair. He lived roughly an hour from us in a small community, and Stephen had been hired to paint the exterior of Henry's two-story home. It was arduous work, scraping off the old paint and priming the surface prior to layering fresh coats of eggshell white on it.

At first Stephen figured he had an anxious customer who wanted an excuse, as odd as it was, to oversee his work without being overt about it. He had had customers in the past who had hovered over his every brushstroke, but this one took the cake, candles and all. Finally Stephen couldn't stand it anymore. "Why do you stay out here all day?" he asked. Henry's smile vanished. He rose from the swing, leaned against the post, and cast his eyes skyward as if he would find the answer there. Stephen was startled to see tears forming in the old man's eyes. Finally, Henry found his voice: "I can't stand to stay inside the house for long."

Seeing the puzzled look on Stephen's face, Henry continued: "My wife died over a year ago, and everything in the house reminds me of her." "Oh, gosh, I'm really sorry to hear that," Stephen said. He resisted the temptation to hug this sweet man. Henry motioned for Stephen to come closer. "Do you have a minute?" he asked, opening the back door. "I'll show you what I mean."

Henry proceeded to give a tour of the house, pointing out one prized possession after another, his voice quavering as he relived each moment. "My wife and I bought this lamp when we were on vacation at..." The tour ended up on the back porch, where they sat down on the swing, sipping iced tea. Henry divulged his entire life to Stephen. His wife's cancer. The children he had outlived. The grandchildren who never wrote. When the shadows grew long, it was time for Stephen to leave.

That night Stephen related his experience to me. With tears in my eyes, I scanned the living room, staring at our collection of antiques garnered from years of canvassing small, dusty towns for that perfect bargain. Antiquing was our shared passion. I had never thought about attaching an item's significance to a time or place that Stephen and I had visited. My eyes settled on an owl clock we had bought the day we were pronounced husband and wife. "Do you remember where we got that clock?" I asked. "Stop it. You're going to make me cry," he said. But he already was.

Stephen stretched out the job longer than normal, taking his sweet time with the details. Henry didn't seem to mind. There were days when Henry cut Stephen's work short so they could sit on that back porch swing together, just sipping lemonade and watching time stroll by. About a month following the completion of the job, I overheard Stephen on the phone. "I'll be there in about an hour or so." "Who was that?" I asked when he hung up. "That was Henry Foster." "I thought you were finished with his job." "Well, not exactly," he answered with a sly smile. "I pretended to forget a few things at his house. I just wanted an excuse to go back. To see how he's doing and all."

Stephen continued making excuses to visit Henry until he ran out of excuses. He began visiting his friend just for the sake of visiting. But then the early arrival of our first baby steered our lives in a different direction, and another baby ten months later filled our social calendar. Living in a fixer-upper consumed us as well. Everything outside our home became secondary. Including a sweet old man named Henry Foster.

We don't know how it happened. As we immersed ourselves into our home and our growing family, the years rolled by. We had two more babies, and our house demanded our full attention to accommodate our burgeoning family. Our priorities shifted, and soon

Henry was relegated to the rank of a distant relative. Guilt bubbled up every now and then when we took a moment to study our collection and reminisce about the time we bought a particular piece. Stephen would sigh and say, "I wonder how the old guy is doing."

One Sunday we filled up our gas tank and took to the back roads, soaking up the scenery. We were on the prowl for that perfect bargain. Stephen took a sudden turn. "Where are we going?" I asked. "You'll see." He navigated streets unfamiliar to me, then slowed down in front of one particular house, a two-story structure with plastic toys littering the front yard and Christmas lights, one month out of season, still stapled to the eaves. Several pecan trees arched up behind the home, the winter sun streaming through their bare branches.

"Who lives here, Daddy?" one of our boys inquired. Stephen swallowed a lump in his throat. "I knew a man who used to live here. His name was Henry Foster." "Was he a nice man?" "Yes, Cody, he was a nice man. A very nice man." "Where is he?" Stephen took a deep breath and exhaled slowly. "Well," he finally replied, his eyes watering, "I believe he went on a long vacation with his wife."

—*Jennifer Oliver*

Life as a Grasshopper

"Weatherman says there'll be a killing frost tonight," my husband said as he slipped on his wool jacket. It was September, and a windless chill was spreading itself over our vegetable garden; gunmetal gray clouds blocked the glow of a nearly full moon. "Got the car keys?" he asked.

He drove our car into the meadow and parked it at the edge of the garden. "I'll pick; you store," he said. "As long as the battery lasts, we'll get all but the root vegetables." We worked all night.

In the morning, the shed looked as if it had been decorated for Christmas. Golden tassels of corn accented the buckets of bright crimson tomatoes and piles of deep green Swiss chard. All day we prepared our produce for canning and freezing. Finally, after counting our filled jars and freezer packets as happily and greedily as children count money from the tooth fairy, we fell into bed. Instantly we slept, comfortably secure in the knowledge that our larder was ready for winter.

Whether by sunlight or headlight, there is something about harvesting homegrown crops that provides security to many people.

Perhaps the simple gathering of food—about as primal a labor as one can find—represents some small control over the uncertainties of life.

Preparing for winter—or for the "rainy days" we're always warned about—didn't come naturally to me. As a child, I was the original grasshopper. While others around me picked berries in the hot sun, carefully steered wet clothes through the wringer washer, or summoned up extra helpings of elbow grease to clean house, I was usually busy singing rhymes and telling stories that always ended with a moral.

In spite of the countless times I was teased about being the grasshopper who fiddled all summer and met a terrifying fate in winter, I paid little heed to the needs of tomorrow.

That began to change in grammar school, however, when my teacher gave me a little dark blue bankbook. "Now, if you bring in part of your allowance every week," she promised me, "the numbers in this book will grow. Before you know it, you'll have a lot of money."

Week after week I brought in my pennies, nickels, and dimes. The teacher led me to the principal's office, where someone took my money and bankbook, then returned the book stamped with new numbers in wet, pungent-smelling black ink. Week by week I watched the amounts grow: $.50, $.90, $1.05, $2.75 ... soon columns of long, uneven lines filled the pages.

I don't remember what I bought with the money. I only remember the sudden shock when the new balance read $0.00.

Zero? But it had taken so very long to make all those columns, I thought. Now, with one quick stamp, my bankbook said all my savings were gone.

It was some years before I realized that life itself is like the amounts in the bankbook and the jars in the larder . . . it has a way of getting used up, of disappearing. Through the years I've watched people work and save, desperately determined to stave off those rainy days and long winters that come to us all. They put their very lives on hold while they squirrel away stores.

But today is at hand as well. "Life is what happens while we're busy making plans," singer John Lennon said. Over the years, even though I still feel wealthy when I have a full pantry and do my best to keep those bank numbers growing, I've learned the wisdom of Lennon's words through my own experience and that of others. One friend worked ten years longer at a job she detested so she and her husband could have a little more money, only to lose her husband during the first months of her retirement. Another saved three times for a trip to Disney World, each time putting it off to spend the money on more practical matters—car repairs, taxes, office equipment. Now, after having a stroke, she will never take that trip.

So, as happens to the best of us if we live long enough, I've come full circle. I've returned to a true appreciation of the grasshopper. After all, as workers, we listen to the grasshopper's joyful music and enjoy the entertainment. His fiddling makes our job easier and helps us lighten up when we feel like grumbling. He gives his labor freely so that ours is made more tolerable, even enjoyable. And that grasshopper would have gone to Disney World the first time around, you can bet your compound interest on it.

So many of us miss life while we're gathering stuff. We get caught up in stuff, the big stuff and the small stuff that bogs us down. We save money to buy stuff, cart our stuff around in new cars, build houses to store our stuff. We keep inventing needs for still more stuff all the time. We're so weighed down by our stuff that even if someone handed us a fiddle, we probably wouldn't have a free hand to pick it up and play it. Besides...

I'd have written more here...but I suddenly decided to go on a picnic. If you need me, look among the grasshoppers.

—*K. K. Wilder*

Revelation on a
Pennsylvania Tour Bus

It's happened to all of us. You're dashing into a convenience store for a quick item when you are politely intercepted with something like this: "Excuse me, miss, but I'm in an awful jam. My car broke down, and I need some bus money to get my wife and kids back home. Could you spare five or ten bucks to help us out?"

Groan. I have offered up cash, then felt duped as I imagined the con artist buying a pack of cigarettes and a six-pack of beer as he sniggered at my naivete. And I've refused, too streetwise to fall for that one, yet left with the gnawing unease that I may have neglected to help a person in real need. Either way feels lousy.

The money wasn't the issue. In the span of a lifetime, a dollar here or there is nothing. It's the uncomfortable sense of being damned if you do, damned if you don't. My unsatisfactory solution was to play both sides. I'd give half the time and ignore the other half—until I was blessed with an *aha!* moment while on a tour bus through Pennsylvania Amish country.

The complimentary tour was provided by the hotel. We motored past horse-drawn buggies and through farmland with no electrical or phone lines connecting the houses. Our first stop was a quilt shop set in the porch and parlor of a two-story home. Next we parted with some traveler's checks at a bakery selling shoofly pie, friendship bread, and cracker pudding. On our way back to the hotel, we passed an open produce stand. No one tended it, but on the counter next to the peppers and tomatoes and jars of jam and chow chow sat a battered shoebox with a hand-lettered sign: "Honor System. Please take what you need and leave payment here."

One of the bus passengers voiced the question many of us were thinking: "What's to keep someone from just taking the food or the money?"

The tour guide said, "It's time to shuck and stack the corn, so all hands are needed. Anyway, the Amish believe that if someone steals from them, it's not their problem. It's the thief's problem."

The casual answer held immense wisdom for me. Eastern religions hold forth about karma, the belief in cosmic checks and balances. And the Bible says that we all have to answer for ourselves on Judgment Day. Either way, theoretically, we are each responsible for our own actions.

This understanding changed the way I feel about the handouts. When I give money, I'm doing the right thing, and that's what matters. Whether or not I'm being conned is really irrelevant—to me, anyway.

Now, that's not to say that I'm stupid about it. I'm not going to give someone standing outside a liquor store a five-dollar bill. I might give him a fast-food gift certificate, though. Nor do I go around holding my purse open. But on the occasion when I feel called upon to be generous, I can be. And I feel good about it.

So I brought back from Amish country a release from a moral dilemma. That, and a hankering for shoofly pie now and then.

—April Burk

PART II

DON'T SWEAT THE SMALL STUFF IN LOVE AND MARRIAGE

Static on the Line

My girlfriend Laura and I are two busy professionals who often try to squeeze as much productivity out of every moment as possible. We both log many minutes on our cell phones and frequently use them to talk to each other on the run. We have had recurring frustration with this, because when you're having a conversation on a cell phone with someone else who is also on a cell phone, the connection can be poor and frequently interrupted with static. At times the connection can be so bad the call is completely lost. It's an empty feeling to be talking to someone and not realizing for a while that she's no longer there and you have been talking to dead air.

Initially, we were so excited to talk to each other that we would try to connect with each other while on the run. However, over time, depending on our moods, we have developed a tendency to snap at each other and say, "Why do you even bother to call me from your cell? Why don't you wait until you get home?"

I travel a good deal. One of these frustrating nonconnections happened on a night while I was traveling in the Baltimore area for a speaking engagement the next day. Laura called me from a fast food restaurant, and due to the static on the line and the background noise in the restaurant, we could barely hear each other. I let the noise overcome my excitement at hearing her voice, and I snapped at her, "Why don't you call me tomorrow?" and hung up. It was a Monday night, September 10, 2001.

We are all aware of the national tragedy that occurred the next day, and as you can imagine, my speaking engagement was interrupted. I quickly learned I would not be flying home to Massachusetts anytime soon. When I got back to the hotel, no calls could get through to Massachusetts, since all the phone circuits were full. I couldn't get through to Laura or any of my other loved ones on the hotel phone. Then I used my cell phone. It was originally supposed to be only a one-day trip, so I didn't have my charger with me, and only a quarter of the battery life was left. I would have given anything to hear her voice and know that Laura was okay, through static or not. In fact, at that point, I longed for the static. Anything would have been better than the silence.

Eventually we did connect again, and when we did, we just laughed about the static. The static was now insignificant, a truly small thing, meaningless in the greater scheme of things. I was actually embarrassed to admit that I would sweat it over the static when I later heard the stories of people trapped under rubble using their cell phones to guide rescuers to their location. Would *they* care if there was static?

This experience reminded me that there is lots of static in life, lots of little things that we can choose to focus on and be magnified in our experience or simply listen right through to what is really important—a loving voice at the other end of the line.

—*Kevin Stacy*

The Best-Laid Plans

I hate to admit it, but once upon a time, I wasn't a very good wife. One of the most embarrassing examples is when I was pregnant with my third child. See, I had the whole birth planned out. It was supposed to be this blissful, heavenly experience. My older girls would stay with my in-laws while we went to the hospital. The nursery would be ready, names would be picked out, my bag would be packed, and every possible contingency would be covered. Everything was supposed to be smooth and trouble-free. I would get to the hospital in plenty of time, have a quick, easy delivery, and everything would be perfect. My room would be filled with flowers and cards. And when I finally held my precious baby, I would be smiling and radiant, extolling the miracle of birth.

Sounds like a lovely fantasy, doesn't it? One you might have had yourself. Needless to say, plans like this are meant to fail. Not one thing went the way I wanted it to. I was angry and upset, and you can be sure I took it out on my husband. Things started going wrong when we went to my in-laws' house for dinner. I wasn't able to eat because I started having pains. I told my husband that we should stay over, because their house was closer to the hospital. He didn't agree. He was tired. He wanted to go home, put the kids to bed, and relax.

This night just wasn't working out. All the way home I was getting more uncomfortable and more irritable. My husband thought I was just overtired and needed some rest. He got the kids settled in for the night and came to check on me. My contractions were ten minutes apart by this time. "Get the kids up and get them back in the car!" I yelled. We had to take them back to his folks' house so we could go to the hospital. All this running back and forth was making me crazy, and I ended up forgetting the bag I had so carefully packed with all of those things I'd need during my perfect delivery.

As we raced to the hospital, my contractions got closer together. Now they were only four minutes apart. I was crying and swearing. If he had done things my way, this wouldn't be happening. "I'll never forgive you if I have this baby in the car!" I wailed. He didn't even get upset; he just squeezed my hand and told me everything would be all right. I didn't want to hear it. Everything I planned so carefully was falling apart, and it was clearly all his fault. For one thing, the crib at home wasn't even set up. And another thing—we couldn't agree on any names. And now I was going to have the baby on the way to the hospital!

Well, it didn't happen that way. In fact, by the time we got there, my contractions were becoming irregular. They would come hard and fast for a while, then subside. The doctor considered sending me back home. That's when I started crying again. Since we lived over an hour away, he finally decided I should stay. He also decided to "help my labor along." Oh, no! This was not what I wanted! I couldn't believe this was happening, and I blamed it on my husband. I tried to make him feel as guilty as I possibly could in between contractions. Soon I was overwhelmed by pain and exhaustion. I didn't even have the energy to abuse my poor husband anymore.

Besides, I really needed him at the moment. I had a lot of nerve expecting him to take care of me after the way I treated him, but you know what? He was wonderful. He did his level best to keep me calm. He stayed by my side every second. He did all he could to soothe me even when I swore at him. He comforted me when I hurt, held me when I cried, and constantly reassured me. Although nothing had gone the way I thought it should, the birth of my daughter was an amazing experience. She was healthy and beautiful. I have never felt closer to my husband. He looked at me with so much love in his eyes; I knew he had forgiven me for being so hateful. He never said a word about the way I acted...he just told me how proud he was of me.

We brought a new life into the world that day, but it breathed new life into our marriage too. I saw my husband—really saw him —for the first time. His patience, forgiveness, and unconditional love helped me realize what was really important. All my perfect plans didn't mean a thing. Having a healthy child and a safe delivery with the man I love by my side was all that mattered. How did I spend so much time with this man and fail to see how special he was? How could I have been so horrible to him just because things didn't go my way? I really don't know, but if I'm lucky, he'll let me spend the rest of my life making it up to him.

— *Sherry Holetzky*

The Path of Worry

It was a perfectly ordinary day, a day like any other. It was a Sunday, so my husband Gene and I went shopping. He had an errand to run at the mall—picking up a pair of running shoes that had been on order for a month. He wears a 10 EEEE, which is not a size you can pluck off the shelf at a shoe store.

And it was a perfectly ordinary night, too. We had leftovers for dinner while we watched something mindless on the tube. Gene promised that starting tomorrow, he'd take the whole week off to help me with some planned events the following weekend. He owned his own company, so it was easy for him to set his own schedule as needed.

As we sat there side by side on the couch, I couldn't concentrate on the show, but began worrying about the plans for the coming weekend. So many guests, so much to do. Who was coming? When were they arriving? Was everything in order for the reception? Should I talk to the caterer one more time? Would everyone show up who had promised to come? Would they be on time? Did I have the right dress? What if… My mind spun with so many details, all of which seemed so critical at the time. How could I have known as I sat there next to Gene on the couch that my life was about to change?

For years, Gene's weekday routine was the same: get up at sunrise, make coffee, go for a run through the hills of our neighborhood, come home and have coffee while reading the paper, shower and face the day. He encouraged me to sleep in and always carefully closed the bedroom door when he left for his run.

This Monday, Gene got up early—before five—and began his routine. Fortunately, he'd completed it through the "come home" part.

At 5:07 A.M. I was suddenly wide awake and running down the hall from our bedroom to the kitchen. I had not heard any noise, but I just knew I had to get to the kitchen. The sliding door to the deck was open a few inches and Gene was lying on the floor between the sliding door and the kitchen table. I grabbed the phone and dialed 911, sticking the phone under my chin while I shoved the table and chairs away (now I know the meaning of adrenaline rush) so I could get to Gene. He wasn't breathing and there was no pulse. The emergency operator was talking to me while I was positioning Gene to prepare to do CPR. No one had warned me how hard it would be to move 180 pounds of deadweight. The longest six minutes of my life began as I tried to keep my husband alive.

I began CPR while I was talking on the phone, putting it down only when I was providing him with air. The anonymous voice on the phone was calm. She down my pace a bit, and when I screamed at her, "Where are they?" she took no offense, but just kept talking me through the process. It seemed like hours before the EMTs arrived, but they were there in only six minutes. One took me aside and asked me questions while the others took care of Gene.

We are lucky, Gene and I. It has been said that if one is going to have a cardiac arrest, the best place for it to happen is in King County, Washington, so we were among the fortunate. The EMTs got him to the hospital in time, where he had bypass surgery and recovered quickly. Today, over a decade later, Gene is thriving. He is doing research on renewable fuels and averaging more than a patent a year.

Although I wouldn't wish this frightening experience on anyone, in some ways I am glad it happened. All those trivial things I was consumed by for much of my life, like the thoughts I'd had the night before Gene's heart attack, have long since been put in perspective for me. When something goes wrong, when my mind begins to wander down the path of worry, I stop and ask myself— wait, is this truly important? Is it life-threatening? No? Then relax. Sit back and watch the show.

—*Jan Lightner*

This Old Cab

It's not often that I run across a well-aged bottle of wine in our house. My husband and I enjoy wine with our dinner and keep the wine closet well stocked with a variety of California wines. This past weekend I began my annual spring cleaning, and instead of sorting out my bath towels by size and color or organizing the boys' school clothes, I decided to turn my attentions to the kitchen cupboards. Kneeling down and peering into the cabinet where we keep our wine, I noticed that it was much deeper than I'd realized. Quite a bit deeper, in fact, and there seemed to be some wine stuck way, way back there. Curious, I leaned in and reached as far back as I could. My fingers just brushed against cold glass. I stretched farther, farther, and yes! My dusty efforts were rewarded with not one, but two bottles I'd never seen before. Old wine? Really old wine.

I held two bottles of wine from the 1970s. "Honey, where'd these come from?" I asked as my husband George came in to refill his coffee cup. Taking the bottles from me, he examined the labels. "I remember buying these at the vineyard's tasting room in Napa. I'd just moved here from Ohio in 1981, and when I bought these bottles they were already five years old. It made me feel very grown-up to be buying vintage wine. Appellations, vintages, it was all pretty heady stuff for a Midwestern boy."

"Can we still drink it?" I asked, not certain how well a twenty-five-year-old bottle would have held up in the back of a closet. "Let's give it a try. If it smells bad, we can use it in the salad."

That afternoon as I planned our dinner, my mind wandered back to the wine. How would that old bottle taste? Wine does improve with age, but it needs to be taken care of, properly stored. Older wines have deeper, richer flavors. Much like the way a marriage deepens and grows, I thought, as I put a roast in the oven. Properly cared for, marriage can be as satisfying and full-bodied as the heartiest of red wines.

How was the wine? I didn't pour it into the salad dressing. It was not a rich, full cabernet sauvignon, but it was certainly still a fruity one. We drank it, raising our glasses high and toasting the fact that two decades before, a young Ohio boy had bravely moved west, where he'd met me.

"So, is this the California life you were dreaming of twenty years ago?" I asked George the next morning as we worked to demolish the redwood deck behind our house (of about the same vintage as the wine we'd opened). My husband, wise enough not to disappoint a sweaty woman holding a crowbar in her hand, smiled broadly. "This is exactly the life I had in mind."

—*Julia Berenson*

It Isn't *Always* About Me

The door slammed, and my husband Rodger walked into the room, a dark look on his face as he glanced in my direction. What could have happened? Was it me? Something I had done?

I tried to become invisible as my mind raced through the litany of things I could have done to cause such a stormy mood. A list of possible defenses and justifications for myself and my actions rose up from inside of me. I quickly surmised what I might do to calm him down. Rodger was quiet, but the air around us was sharp. Finally I couldn't resist asking the same question he had heard many times before. "Are you upset with me?"

This was a scene from our marriage that was repeated over and over. If the answer was "Yes, I am angry with you," he would do it in a tight, angry way. I would immediately respond like a wounded animal that needed to defend itself. If the answer was "No, it's not you," but instead something that had happened at work, or as a result of other people or situations, I would immediately want to make him feel better by taking on his feelings, his indignation, his stress—and then dishing out advice on how to make it all better.

Deep down I knew this was a negative pattern we were falling into. I could feel his resentment, and I could also sense that I was giving away some part of myself through these interactions.

So every time Rodger was in a bad mood, my first reaction was to feel responsible for it — I must have done something wrong. Most of the time his mood had nothing to do with me, but it affected me anyway.

But now, after many more years of marriage, I have learned to avoid this track. I now realize that his moods are determined by nobody but him, no matter what. I have also accepted the reality that many things happen in his life that have nothing to do with me, and working his feelings out about all of those things is his job, not mine.

Even if he actually is grumpy about some issue currently brewing between us, his decision about when and where to vent his feelings is his choice. No matter what may have happened, no one but Rodger can make Rodger feel any given way. This was such a tough concept to grasp — it probably took three years of practicing before I actually believed and acted on it.

However, once I understood this, many amazing things happened. Since I no longer felt responsible, I also no longer felt defensive. Once I let go of needing to control and fix his feelings, he became much more comfortable being honest with me about why he felt various ways. With each new experience we discover that even really deep, difficult issues can be openly discussed (mostly) rationally. The land mines have been defused, and I have regained strength and self-respect. Rodger respects me more, and we can deal with our lives separately and jointly in a calmer, more peaceful manner.

The most amazing thing is that our love for each other has grown beyond what we had ever experienced before. It must be that by letting go of the need to control him, I am honoring Rodger for the incredible and self-possessed individual he is.

Now, when he chooses to bring a black cloud into the house at the end of the day, I just smile, turn around, and release Rodger's energy back to him with a big, deep refreshing breath. If he wants to talk about it, I know he'll let me know.

—*Clare Benoit*

Goodbye, Ruby Tuesday:
A Valentine Story

"Hi, hon! How about going out for lunch today?" It was my husband Michael, calling home from work with an invitation that was tempting but not practical. "I don't know," I tried to remind him. "You remember what happened the last time we tried to take Grant out for lunch this close to naptime."

Our last attempt at anything fancier than McDonald's lunchtime playroom ended rather abruptly in a local Greek restaurant where our two-year-old son had a grand mal toddler meltdown. He was way beyond tired and, it turned out, possessed a definite dislike for the cuisine that was powerful enough to overcome the allure of getting to color on their swanky paper tablecloths. Of course, we also noticed no one smiled at or spoke to the little guy, and it appeared they had only one combination booster seat/high chair in the entire ultra-contemporary eatery. My guess is they weren't catering to small fry. I suppose had I been only two feet tall with a small vocabulary and no nap, I'd have felt unsettled there, too.

After that fiasco, we resolved to stick with ordinary grilled cheese and soup and the more kid-friendly atmosphere of our own home for our noontime dates. But it seems that the memory of that day had faded somewhat for my husband.

"Aww, c'mon. It's Valentine's Day," Michael pleaded, "and we'll go somewhere he'll be more comfortable. We have those gift certificates for Ruby Tuesday's. Let's use those."

Reluctantly, I finally agreed. Maybe it was the idea of a free meal that made it so enticing. . . .

I picked Michael up from his office and we drove to Ruby Tuesday's. Luckily, the lunch crowd had thinned, so we weren't pressured to hurry or forced to wait extra time for our table (these things really matter when you're dining with a toddler). No sooner had we walked in, though, than the host happily handed Grant a helium-filled balloon. Someday I am going to track down and flog the person responsible for coming up with the nutty idea of giving children helium balloons in restaurants. It must have been someone without children. And so began an endless ritual of retrieving the bobbing latex bubble from the ceiling as it conveniently slipped from Grant's grasp, making its way clear across the room. It floated and bounced above the tables of other diners as it traveled, stopping when it became entangled in an occasional light fixture, where we would quickly snatch it down, only to repeat the whole process again about thirty seconds later.

When we weren't chasing the balloon, we did get to eat. And the food was very tasty, even when eaten very quickly (a skill every parent develops for dining with a toddler). Grant, however, tired of his meal much sooner than we did, so in a creative effort to pass the time while his parents learned to chew faster, he suddenly slithered down under the table and snaked his way past our feet until he found freedom.

Crawling at full speed across the floor (I didn't know he could still do that), he dashed under other tables and rolled under nearby chairs like a James Bond wanna-be, much to the amusement of the other patrons (but NOT of his parents). Their innocent chuckles and smiles only encouraged his rogue behavior. He had an audience and knew how to work the crowd. When we'd finally catch him, he'd just let his little body go limp like a cat and giggle as we tried to literally fold him into position again at the table.

This just wasn't working, Valentine's Day be darned. Exhausted and defeated, we decided to end the torture and head for home (another useful skill for parents: admitting defeat).

When the waitress finally brought the bill, Michael said with a grin, "Uh, you got any money?" The bill was slightly more than the value of our gift certificates. No, actually, I didn't have any money with me. And he didn't either, having left his wallet behind at his office once I'd arrived with the certificates.

"That's okay," I said without a worry or second thought, "I have my bank card. How short are we?" "Ninety-two cents," Michael replied with a laugh. A scene flashed before my eyes as I opened my purse. It was a mental picture of my putting my bank card on the breakfast bar earlier that morning. The mental picture ended there, though. I hadn't put my card back *into* my wallet.

Blushing, I began fumbling around the bottom of my purse for loose change. But now another memory floated up—me deciding not long ago to clean out my purse and deposit all that pesky loose money into the change bucket at home!

My husband and I began to giggle. Concerned, the waitress came over to ask if everything was okay (I think she was watching me remove everything from my purse and billfold). We smiled and reassured her all was well. When she walked away, we furiously dove into our coat and pants pockets in search of whatever coinage we could scrape together. Our last resort would be the car; there might be some loose change under the seats. Surely between us we could scrounge together ninety-two cents!

Our dignity was saved that day. Without going to the car, we finally found just enough—mostly pennies. We paid the tab and raced out of the building as fast as we could to avoid further embarrassment, while I made a mental note to add Ruby Tuesday's to my list of restaurants where we should probably never show our faces again.

The wind put the finishing touches on the romantic Valentine's Day outing as it snatched poor Grant's red balloon and whisked it away into the gray, misty sky. Such a very memorable lunch with my two handsome dates, definitely one I'll never forget! I don't think it was quite what Michael had in mind, though, because now when he calls home and invites us to have lunch with him, he always just asks with a chuckle, "And what would you guys like me to order from McDonald's?"

—*Amanda Krug*

Letting Go

I thought he was the man of my dreams. So when we abruptly broke up, I was angry and heartbroken—this was not the plan.

We were on track to a future together, I wanted to believe, but in the back of my mind, I knew this needed to happen. My boyfriend and I had been together for several years, living together in an adorable little house he owned, but that we'd chosen together. It was a perfect beginning to the next stage of our life: walls filled with windows so the light could stream in on the hardwood floor, a huge yard for our two puppies to play in, and in a very peaceful country setting with lots of honeysuckle, rosebushes, and maple trees.

We painted the entire interior together and decorated everything exactly the way we wanted it. We had many memorable days, playing with the dogs in the yard, cleaning the house together while listening to our favorite music, throwing big barbecue parties with friends, spending holidays with family, and best of all—stepping into the warmth of the sauna after long, hard bike rides. How was it possible that I was now closing that heavy green door behind me one last time, glancing back at all of those windows just one last time? I pulled the heavy door closed on that part of my life and set off.

I truly thought he was the one for me. And he thought I was the one for him. Toward the end, though, it became clear, in small ways and in some very big ways, too, that we just weren't right for each other. After we broke up and I had had some time to grieve, it became clear to me that everything was happening for a perfect reason. I realized that everything had God's fingerprints on it, and what seemed like a tragic mistake was really a blessing in disguise.

I let go; I stopped focusing on a memory, and turned to the dreams I'd had all along. In the year I've been on my own, I've been able to focus on me, on my goals. I have lived by myself for the first time in my life. At long last I am graduating from college and will embark on the next phase of my career. I'm leaving for a big European vacation on my own! Just me and my passport, with no one left behind. I can hardly remember that there was a time not so long ago when the idea of leaving for two weeks—of leaving him—was unimaginable.

I do believe it was destiny for us to meet and spend the years we did together; it was a part of the perfect plan. There will be another loving partner in my life, I am certain. My soul mate is out there; I know now that I won't settle for less in love. When will I find my true love? He is certain to arrive sometime while I'm busy living for my dreams.

—*Stella Black*

Honeymoon at Last

My wife Christa and I had been planning a vacation to New Mexico for several months. All four of our daughters were scheduled for spring break vacations — giving my wife and me our first extended time alone since we had gotten married. We were married in front of a justice of the peace during our lunch hour and hadn't even taken a honeymoon!

We had both struggled through much of the first two years of our marriage to establish a new relationship with each other, and for me to adjust to the four wonderful stepdaughters I inherited. Basic housekeeping details for such a large family left us with very little time to give just to each another (so we thought), and we were faltering in the already difficult steps of a new marriage.

The vacation had become our soul (pun intended) point of focus. We had planned it to be unplanned: to just go where the wind blew us, sleeping wherever we got tired and could find shelter, be it hotel, campsite, or side of the road. The idea was to have only each other to rely on—a true adventure. The simple, stark beauty of New Mexico called to us.

Less than two weeks before we left, I took the car in to be tuned up and checked over. We knew the car needed some repairs and wanted it to be in excellent condition for the trip through mountains and desert. The mechanic called, and after working with him to establish what the bare minimum repairs needed to be, we came up with a bill of several hundred dollars, not including the timing belt! Instantly I realized we could no longer afford to make the trip if we fixed the car, and we certainly couldn't risk having it break down on us in the middle of the desert. I phoned my wife at work and shared the bad news.

We were both bitterly disappointed. It seemed the final straw in what we perceived to be a tremendously stressful life. Our escape from the cares of everyday life had vanished, and with it an opportunity to renew our relationship. These were no ordinary vacation plans, weighted with all the hope we had invested in them, and we were devastated. We felt we had once again been had by fate, as this opportunity to revitalize was dangled just out of reach. The travel guides we had bought now seemed to taunt us.

How could we salvage our plans? We try not to sweat the small stuff in our lives, but hey, this seemed to be really big stuff. Well, was it really, though? Was our marriage really hanging on our making this trip? After all, we would have taken our problems with us, and the reality was, we had only each other to rely on anyway.

We decided that we could still afford to take time off from work and have a mini-vacation at home. We were, after all, now freed up for six unstructured days of time together, and could afford several small things we had put off doing because of the vacation.

Instantly I began to feel better. The vacation had been the one thing I looked forward to that got me through all of the difficulties of the past few months. But I very decided that I had better reframe things and look forward to this new time off, or I could become depressed.

Through a series of e-mails, my wife and I went from arguing about the situation to a resolution to light a proverbial candle and not curse the darkness. We determined to work hard on looking forward to this new vacation and decided we might even be better off, because we wouldn't be absorbed in the logistics of the trip and could focus squarely on each other.

I love to cook, and we decided we could enjoy gourmet dinners over candlelight. We were free to come and go as the whim took us. We were only fifteen miles from Dallas, Texas, one of the largest cities in the United States, which offered us unlimited options for entertainment: concerts, museums, foreign films, all of the things we love in common. We were having a great time winnowing through many options to tailor the perfect romantic vacation for two—right at home! A slight shift in perspective had made all the difference.

—*Stephen McDermott*

If That's the Worst Thing

While I was growing up, when chaos arrived, Mother would say, "I'll skirt it." Which meant she would take an alternative to the issue. For instance, if her cake fell, she topped it with peaches, strawberries, or a fruit. If a dress became torn, Mother would embroider a flower or an initial over the patch. My father fought turmoil by salvaging the pieces to make a profit. If his car broke down, he didn't sell the car; instead, he sold parts from the car in his shop and received more money than he could have gotten for the car as a whole. A storm hit Papa's tool shed and collapsed it. He sold the lumber and roof for enough money to build a new shed.

But me, I was always in a hurry; I wanted everything fixed now. When Glenn and I decided to marry, we discussed many issues that would ensure our happiness. Of course, my first wish was to have a perfect wedding. Glenn told me to plan whatever would make me happy; he would go along with whatever I desired. My parents and I lived in Doniphan, Missouri, a small Ozark town without a bakery. Glenn lived thirty miles away in the city of Poplar Bluff, Missouri, and his friend operated a bakery. Therefore, Mother ordered the tiered wedding cake and two sheet cakes from his friend's bakery, and the plan was that Glenn would bring the cakes to my parents' home.

On Saturday, before our wedding on Sunday, Glenn brought the wedding cake in the backseat of his car to my parents' house. Mother, Papa, and I stood on the porch to greet him. We didn't notice, however, that another spectator was witnessing the scene....Glenn opened the car door and got out, but before he could slam the door, my dog Rex jumped in. Four humans shouted together, "Rex! No!" But that didn't faze him. He had been overlooked during the wedding plans and preparations, but now he leaped back in the spotlight. He jumped on the back of the driver's seat, then leaped into the backseat right onto the wedding cake. I can still see the little bride and groom ornaments topple from the top of the cake toward the floor of the car. He walked on one sheet cake, then the other. He turned around twice and settled comfortably in the middle of the second cake, panting and looking up at the four frantic people outside the car.

"My wedding!" I cried. "There goes my perfect wedding. What will we do? The bakery is already closed." Mother, Papa, and Glenn stood and looked at Rex on the cake. The dog seemed to snuggle deeper into the cake and looked up at everyone. They began to laugh. Mother said, "At least there's waxed paper over the cakes."

"It's not funny," I yelled. "The bride and groom fell off of the top! Doesn't that jinx Glenn and me?"

Glenn put his arms around me and wiped tears from my cheeks. "I'll call Toll and see if he won't bake a sheet cake and have it ready in the morning. I'll pick it up." Mother said she would bake a white cake. She called Beulah and Georgia, who would serve the cake tomorrow, described the chaos, and asked if they would each bake a white cake and bring it to our house in the morning. After they got through giggling, both agreed. Mother gave Papa and Glenn a list to buy at the grocery store: five 16-ounce cans of easy-to-spread white cake icing and five 12-ounce cartons of whipped cream. She warned them that they might need to go to more than one store to fill the order. We had a party the Saturday night before the wedding, but I was in such a daze about the wedding cake that I never really relaxed and enjoyed it.

On Sunday morning, four hours before the wedding, Mother, Beulah, and Georgia gathered in the dining room and pieced and spliced their cakes and the crushed wedding cakes together with white icing to form sheet cakes. The ladies sculpted whipped cream in the crevices on the lopsided wedding cake until it regained its size. Our bride and groom figurines topped the cake once again, and looked as if they had never toppled the day before.

After our wedding, when all were in the reception room, many women commented, "What a beautiful cake." While they were eating the cake, many said, "This is the first wedding I was ever at where they had whipped cream on the cake. Yum! Good!" No one was ever the wiser. Why would they ever suspect that a dog had been resting on top of the cake just the day before?

"Now, Garnet." Glenn kissed my wedding rings and fingers. "We had a perfect wedding. Let's see that we have a perfect marriage, a perfect life together. My darling wife, just remember: When stuff happens like a dog jumping onto the wedding cake, just think, if that's the worst thing that happens today, it will be a good day." And he was right.

We are now just a few short years away from our fiftieth wedding anniversary. I'm already making plans for the cake….

—*Garnet Hunt White*

It's All in How You View It

Years ago, I was waiting for what I considered to be an important phone call from my agent. He had left a message the night before telling me that three shows that I had been booked for were now canceled, and that a television show I was in the running for now looked bleak.

I had called my agent back early the next day. He wasn't available, though; his secretary told me he was in a meeting and assured me that he would call me the minute the meeting was over.

So I waited. And waited. Three hours dragged by and still no call.... I called again. This time his secretary told me he was out to lunch. I hung up, angry. All kinds of negative thoughts were going through my head. Now, when a thought, negative or positive, is going through my head, I have a tendency to speak that thought out loud as I pace back and forth. You can imagine the scene....

The hours dragged by, the thoughts piled up. It didn't take long before I had convinced myself that not only didn't my agent care about my career, he didn't care about me.

At this point I was overwhelmed by negativity. I started talking to the phone. Let me make that statement clear—I wasn't talking *on* the phone, I was talking *at* the phone. "Let me wait, will you? I don't deserve this kind of treatment! Who do you think you are!" Even the dogs looked at me as if to say, *Don't you have to pick the phone up first?*

As I talked to the phone, I didn't realize my wife was taking in this little scene. Without missing a beat she stepped in front of me, grabbed the phone, disconnected the wires from the desk, and started yelling at the phone. "Yeah! Who do you think you are, treating my husband like that? Bad telephone! Bad telephone!" And she swept it up off the desk and threw it in the garbage.

I stood watching her, speechless. What on earth...? "Honey, what are you doing?" I asked.

"Well, I don't know what this phone did to upset you," she said calmly, "but whatever it was, it will no longer stay in this house." She looked around my office. "Is the fax machine bothering you, too? How about the computer? Because if they are, I won't tolerate it!" She stepped to the doorway of the office and yelled into the rest of the house: "Now hear this! Can I have your attention, please? All of the appliances, furniture, and other inanimate objects in this house—if you do anything to upset my husband, out you go! This is the law! I have spoken!" Then she quietly walked away.

She was back as quickly as she'd left. Plucking the telephone out of the trash can, she said to it, "You're not so tough now, are you?" Then she turned to me, kissed me on the cheek, patted my head, and said, "You see, honey, you just have to learn how to take control." And with that, she left the room.

After watching a crazy woman running through the house on a rampage, yelling at everything in sight, I noticed that something in my mood had changed. I was laughing. The question is, Why was I laughing at a situation that moments before had made me emotionally distraught? The answer, of course, is that my wife had helped me realize I was sweating the small stuff. Her antics pulled me away from this negative situation and let me see myself as the star in a scene from my own comedy. And yes, twenty minutes later my agent did call. I was able to listen to him and tell him my concerns—without the anger and frustration that had been building up earlier. And you know what? We haven't ever had any more trouble with that phone!

—*Steve Rizzo*

In Sickness and in Health

There is a framed wedding photo on my desk. I like to position it so that I can see the beaming face of the bride. No, it isn't a picture of me; my wedding photo is over on the windowsill. This is a photo of my best friend Laura Lewis, the day she and her husband Pete were married for the second time.

"We're going to Jamaica. Pete and I are planning to have another wedding ceremony to renew our vows," she told me on the phone one summer afternoon. "Would you guys like to come along?" Go to Jamaica? Heck, who wouldn't want to go to Jamaica?

Well, me, for one. This was a trip that I knew would be difficult. Yes, Jamaica is lovely. Yes, the hotel is great. Yes, I like the beach. But I knew why Laura was planning this trip, and it made me want to lie down on the floor and cry. At the tender age of thirty-six, the mother of two young children, she had just been told that the breast cancer for which she'd been treated two short years earlier had returned. This trip was to be her reward for undergoing yet another round of chemotherapy. The thought of lying on the beach in Jamaica would give her something to focus on during those long and painful hours. No, it wasn't a lighthearted trip by any means, but of course I would go.

And her plans to renew their vows? That was done for a reason, too. "We wrote our vows the first time we were married," she told me in her lilting British voice. "And I left out the part about 'in sickness and in health.' I think it's high time I snuck that part back in, don't you think?" And she giggled.

Our two families traveled down to Jamaica together and checked into a family resort. While the children played on the beach and our husbands tried to windsurf, Laura and I met with the wedding consultant to pick out a cake and order champagne. Later that same afternoon, we sat by the pool and I took careful notes as she shared her funeral plans with me.

It was a beautiful tropical wedding. My husband and I watched as the minister read the marriage service aloud. Our two boys stood with Laura and Pete's children, watching the ceremony in silent awe. They'd never seen a wedding before.

"You may kiss the bride," the Jamaican minister announced, and Pete grabbed his wife and kissed her with passion. The children looked away in embarrassment, but I wasn't surprised. They'd carried on like newlyweds throughout their marriage, long before they knew she was sick. No problem, big or small, seemed to faze them. Life was met with a perpetual smile and a hearty laugh.

Laura died a year after that Jamaican ceremony, in November of 2000. She was thirty-seven. In the picture I keep on my desk, Laura looks radiant. She stands on a balcony high over the ocean and looks straight at the camera with a wide smile, a bald bride holding a large bouquet of pink and white flowers. When I study the picture, I can pretend to myself that my friend is nearby, looking at me and smiling. But I know who she was looking at. She was looking at Pete.

—*Jennifer Basye Sander*

Letting Go by Accident

My dad called on the cell phone just as we started to fishtail in our fourteen-foot U-Haul. My husband Matt was driving, our dog Noah sitting between us. I don't remember dropping the phone while repeating "OH MY GOD" as the truck slid into the median and flipped over on its side. We lay perfectly still in about five feet of snow.

Noah stood next to Matt's head, licking the window. I was trembling, my entire weight balanced on Matt's shoulder and hip. The phone dangled over our heads from the cord plugged into the cigarette lighter. After a few minutes, it rang. It was my dad calling back. Matt assured him that we were fine. Stunned and shaking, but fine.

Later, as a tow truck slowly tipped our U-Haul upright, we heard everything we owned crashing from one side to the other— metal clunks from the bed frame or my bike, maybe. Loose boxes landing with staccato thuds. And the unmistakable sound of ceramic pots and glasses breaking .

I remembered a bus accident I had witnessed in China. The passengers were okay, but stranded now in the frozen tundra of a northern province. It looked as though the bus had tipped over when it had tried to circumvent a broken-down truck. Three men attempted to straighten the axle on the truck with a crowbar. A few more worked to upend the bus. In this remote mountain area, we could not expect any tow trucks or emergency highway help. It seemed that our bus would have to wait until the wreck could be cleared.

I was traveling with three Westerners, friends I had made on a horse trek the week before. We gathered red peppers that had spilled from the truck. The sweet scent of parsley that had also tumbled to the ground filled the air, so strong it seemed to create a cloud in a muted shade of green.

Far off, we made out the shapes of great hairy yaks and a horse with red tassels on his harness. We could also see smoke coming from a white yurt. I worried about what might happen at sundown. A few of the Chinese seemed content to gather around small fires.

We weren't outside for more than an hour when we heard our bus starting up. Our foolhardy bus driver decided to drive the bus around the wreck. We turned to watch, wide-eyed. The bus rocked hard to the left. A dog that was up with the luggage on top suddenly stood. Another swing to the right flung him from the roof. He hung by a rope alongside the windows.

The Chinese seemed indifferent, but my friend Clélie started jumping and squealing, "Le chien, le chien, mon dieu!" In the dour voice of a BBC reporter, my other friend Steve began narrating the events for his video camera. I had begun to cry.

The bus driver ground the engine in first gear to veer sharply onto the road again, having barely cleared the accident. Miraculously, the dog clambered back up. Within minutes, the driver motioned to us to climb aboard. We continued on our journey north.

I don't know how long the others waited in the cold, whether they made it home, or what they lost. I don't know if they would have mourned the dog had he choked to death. I wondered if perhaps the Chinese travelers were less attached to their possessions. Maybe they were more adaptable to hardship than I was.

After our U-Haul accident, Matt and I drove two more days to make it to our new apartment in Seattle. We kept experiencing the illusion that we were sliding again, especially along the Columbia River in Oregon.

Even now, I shudder when I think that we could have gone off the other side of the highway, down the steep, icy cliff. We had no control once we hit the ice. We were merely lucky. I feel pain in my heart when I think of my dad hearing his daughter scream and then silence.

Around the house, there are telltale signs of our wreck—nicks on the bookshelves, a bend in the wrought-iron standing lamp, and a crack in a Woody Allen photo from *Love and Death*. And when I vacuum the area rugs, curry powder still wafts up from an upended spice rack.

Of course I wouldn't think of storing my dog with the luggage; now I don't care as much when a glass slips off the kitchen counter and smashes to bits. I often go to whoever is within reach—my husband or my dog—clasp his head in my palms, and say, "It's okay. We're fine."

—*Leslie M. Duss*

Grumpy Comes,
and Grumpy Goes

On a beautiful spring day, as the temperature climbed over fifty degrees, I bundled up in my sweater and went out for a walk in the neighborhood. I was feeling out of sorts and hoped that the fresh air would help to clear my mood.

I admit it—as a sensitive woman, I am greatly influenced by the moods of my husband and our children. No matter what mood I wake up in, if my children are cranky and they don't like my toast, or my husband is disgruntled about something, my mood can shift instantly from cheery to troubled. Even when what is wrong with those around me has nothing to do with me, I try to fix it, feel responsible for causing it, or feel melancholy because those I love are down. I suspect I'm not the only wife and mother who feels this way.

I'd left the house that afternoon because my husband was in a cranky mood, and it pained me to see it. As I walked around the neighborhood, God sent me a little message to help lighten my mood. It was written in the sky.

I watched an airplane flying above me, leaving a trail of white smoke behind it. This looked so permanent, a wide white slash across the sky. Then, within a matter of moments, the jet trail dissipated, leaving no trace that the smoke was ever there.

Weren't moods like that? Weren't many problems as illusory as jet smoke? I imagined that the jet trails were my husband, scowling and spewing negativity. The image made me laugh. Here I was, getting all worked up about my husband's bad mood, when it was only a bunch of air and gas that would disappear in a matter of moments or hours.

I shifted my gaze to the clear blue sky that surrounded the airplane. I took a deep breath, felt the sunshine on my face, listened to the beautiful music of birds chirping, admired the colorful flowers blooming all over the neighborhood, and drank in the beauty of the cool green grass. Life gives us choices—I could choose to focus on a thousand miracles all around me or on the clouds that would soon disappear. Which would it be?

It was a no-brainer. The miracles won. Why sweat the small stuff when there is beauty all around me and I can find inspiration in the sky? By the time I returned home, my husband was smiling again. And his smiles last much longer than smoke.

—Azriela Jaffe

Acid Rain

Is there a time more peaceful than the end of the day, when dusk slowly turns into twilight? This is that time when my husband Bill and I like to relax on our deck with something cool to drink, listening to the music of the evening and sharing the events of our day. Throughout the years, it has become our favorite time together.

During one of these pleasant evenings, my husband mentioned casually that our deck really needed a face-lift and that the fence could stand replacing. I readily agreed, and the next week we dove straight into our new project. We power-washed, cleaned, and prepared for the next phase. The do-it-yourself home store in our neighborhood became a regular stopping point whenever we were out. Fence and deck manuals were purchased, and paint samples began to collect by the dozens on our dining room table. As we pored over designs and ideas, our project began to take shape.

We both knew this was to be no ordinary deck and fence. Our design called for latticework at the top, with each of the sections to be in framework, and the old railings torn away in preparation for a more open look. By the next week the fence boards were delivered, the two-by-fours purchased, the latticework and hardware selected. This was shaping up quickly, I thought to myself. Remarkably, we'd agreed on every detail. Every project in a marriage should proceed so smoothly!

It was time to begin building. We spent almost every afternoon and weekend on our project. I helped as much as I could, but truthfully, my husband was the builder, craftsman, and artisan. I watched him in amazment, and told him I thought he could do anything. With Bill working away and me looking on with pride, this deck project was humming along. Perhaps I should begin planning a deck-warming party to celebrate in the weeks ahead? But no. Just as the end was in sight, our détente collapsed. The paint did us in.

We discussed textures and colors with experts. We compared notes. We did everything but agree. He wanted one thing, I wanted another. Clearly the choice should be mine, I believed. After all, I had already chosen what I wanted. Case closed, end of discussion! Unfortunately, a decorator at the home store disagreed with me. This person, a so-called expert on the subject, explained to me that paint would weather, chip, and peel after about two years. My husband's choice of a translucent stain was the way to go. It would soak into the wood, thus protecting and preserving it…blah, blah, blah! I was outmaneuvered, and I knew it.

I grumbled all the way home about how much more stain it

would take. "Not only that, it is bound to stink," I added. Once the stain was applied, it did indeed smell, just as I knew it would! This project, once the product of two like minds, had collapsed into petty bickering. I was irritated and remained sullen.

One evening several weeks later, during the six o'clock news, I noticed Bill was not in the den as usual. He was lounging on our new deck. Why hadn't he asked me to join him? I noticed the sky darkening; a summer storm was building and about to break. Shaking my head at his nuttiness, I walked outside to join him.

His eyes were closed, but he wasn't dozing because his patio chair rocked slightly. A powerful lightning bolt seemed to burst into an upward glow, followed by rolling thunder. I could almost taste the rain, and the wind was blowing a mix of cool and warm air. Caught up in the moment, neither of us spoke a word. Although I really wanted to break the silence and comment on how enjoyable the evening felt, I didn't. Instead, I asked in a cynical tone if he was enjoying the still-lingering smell on such a beautiful night. He ignored me. I asked him to just keep his eyes closed and describe that smell to me, "And don't say you don't smell anything!"

His eyes remained closed and almost in another voice, he began a dialogue, as if jolted backward in time. I stopped talking immediately and listened in quiet reverence, because it was not often he spoke of Vietnam. The light show of our evening became exploding mortar fire. The whirling winds became hot and unbearable, rushing through the open doors of an Army gunship on the way to lend air support. And the smell. The smells were overwhelming...blood, fuel, smoke, and death. At that moment I wanted to hold him, but I knew that he would never allow it. In that moment I felt so very ashamed of myself. So ashamed, I wanted to run away and hide my face. What small stuff I had overreacted to! It almost stole the joy and beauty of what we had accomplished together. As I remember that evening, I realize that a higher power was at work, and I am grateful for what I was taught as a result.

—*Lanette A. Suggs*

PART III

DON'T SWEAT THE SMALL STUFF IN PERSONAL GROWTH

The Turtle

As a First Nation Canadian woman of the Amaham band in British Columbia, I have learned that dreams may be a wonderful guide to solving problems that bother me in the waking hours. One dream in particular was so clear and powerful in its message that the memory of it still lingers.

At this particular time I felt exhausted from the turmoil in my life. Stress from my job and struggles in my family had left me exhausted mentally, spiritually, and emotionally. In my dream, I was walking along a beautiful road beside Cultus Lake, the "lake with no bottom." The summer sun was coming down through the giant cedar trees. The summer air was humid and filled with the sounds of children playing, birds singing, and the hum of little creatures.

As I walked slowly down this road, I noticed a little turtle trying to cross it. Worried that a passing car would run the turtle over, I carefully picked it up and returned it to the water's edge. Smiling at my good deed, I stood up. Behind me at the lake's edge there was an Indian Grandmother, standing quietly. I looked around—there was no one else at the lake. She must have come to speak to me.

I waited respectfully for her to speak. Finally she did, asking me why I had taken the turtle from the road and put him by the lake. I responded proudly, "Well, that is where the turtle should be." She smiled and shook her head slowly. Speaking softly, she said, "Do you know how long it took for that little turtle to make its way up to the road?"

Upon waking that morning, I remembered the dream in vivid detail and tried to reflect on its meaning. What could she have meant? Why did she think it was wrong for me to move the turtle?

And then it came to me, the way in which I move turtles all the time. I realized that often in life I am not content just to lead my own life, but I also try to arrange people where I think they should be. Without respecting others' rights to travel at their own speed on their own routes to their destination, I interfere. Not only does it drag on me emotionally, but it also prevents them from learning their own lessons in life. Grandmother's appearance in that dream let me know that I should not interfere with my Earth Brothers' and Sisters' journeys.

—*Desta Tocher*

Flying High

I woke up that morning with a pain in my neck, moaning softly while opening my eyes and trying to grasp just exactly where I was. Alaska. I was in Dillingham on the western coast of Alaska. The bush country, a vast countryside of snow, where there were few roads and fewer people.

I sat up and looked around for Stephen, but he had already left for the airport. Stephen. I leaned back, closed my eyes, and smiled. Now here was a person who could make me laugh and cry at the same time. He could fill my head with such amazing stories about his life that I wondered where reality ended and fantasy had taken over. He had grabbed me with both hands and pulled me out of the shell in which I'd hidden for years. Stephen didn't care what people thought. He spoke, acted, and behaved exactly as he felt. He was neither shy nor afraid, and he certainly didn't sweat life's small stuff. No small stuff at all. There was no middle ground with Stephen: Either you liked the man or you didn't. I loved him with a passion.

The ringing phone brought me back to the moment. I picked up the receiver. "Hello?" "Where the hell are you, Kinky?" Stephen's voice boomed into my ear. "I just got up, and it's taking me a while to get moving," I replied, rubbing the ache in my neck. "Okay, but hurry up. I'm waiting for you in the lounge."

Stephen was a bush pilot. He spent his days flying small planes over isolated stretches of snowy wilderness, carrying mail, supplies, and people from town to town. In a land where the weather patterns changed constantly, the job of bush pilot was not for the weak at heart.

But here I was, having arrived a week ago for the summer. These had been incredible days. I had flown with him every day until about ten P.M., when the rays of the sun melted into the snowy fields. We thrived in each other's company, mixing friendship, passion, and adventure. I loved every minute. Stephen had introduced me to the majestic beauty of Alaska's wilderness. He dropped down low and flew over animal tracks spread out over miles of snow-covered fields. He soared over hills dipped in fog, and my soul floated out of the plane, creating its own flight pattern high above us.

I was very excited about this summer. We would be together, and I would learn to appreciate the rugged beauty of Alaska as Stephen had done for so many years.

I dragged myself into the shower and let the hot water massage the muscles in my neck. The phone rang again. Dripping wet, I ran to answer it. "Why is it taking you so long to get beautiful? Just come on over already!" Stephen laughed and I felt the warmth of his love. "I'm on my way," I assured him.

I pulled a sweater over my head and ran a hand through the curly hair that Stephen had taught me to appreciate. My thoughts wandered back to Berkeley two years ago, when I had first been introduced to Stephen, who was in town with his family, on a break from his pilot's job in Alaska. He had taken me flying around San Francisco, looked me in the eyes, fed me sushi and chocolates, talked to me and encouraged me to talk. I opened up. We had connected emotionally, physically, and spiritually on a level that I never knew possible. I was on a high for two years.

My parents weren't pleased. According to them, Stephen was unrefined, unpredictable, and not stable. At that moment in my life, he was what I needed and was attracted to after years of living in a very controlled environment. Stephen had taught me to love and to be a free spirit. It was hard to let go, to relax—until I met Stephen. How could I give that up for a more responsible and traditional partner?

One evening during a weekend trip through Napa Valley, we settled into a beautiful hotel room and Stephen asked me what I wanted for dessert. "Oh, but it's too late. I can't go downstairs and have chocolate now," I began. "Of course you can't go downstairs. They're closed. We'll order from room service!" He was so confident.

"Room service?" I squeaked. "But it's too expensive." I tried to be sure of myself. Stephen ignored me. "Let's see. Whaddaya want?" He studied the menu.

"I—I don't know," I stammered, still adjusting to the fact that he wanted to order dessert from room service at ten P.M. And that it was okay. I went into the bathroom to brush my teeth, hoping the subject would disappear. When I returned, a large tray had magically appeared on my pillow with not one dessert, but five. That was Stephen. He constantly stretched the boundaries of my existence. Sometimes it was good, but sometimes it felt unsettling.

The phone rang, for the third time. "Okay, Inez, they've got me flying outta here in fifteen minutes. I'll meet you in the lounge or on the runway."

"I'm on my way, Stephen. Don't leave me behind!" I begged. My neck was so stiff. Spasms of pain shot through my shoulders as I ran out of the apartment and headed up the dirt road to the small airport.

"Please wait. Please wait," I whispered urgently as the airport tower came into view. I walked as fast as I could up the steep hill. As I turned into the airport, I debated briefly. Should I check the pilot's lounge or head straight to the airplane? I ran to the runway and came to a halt.

There was his airplane, slowly moving toward the runway. Stephen's face was in the window, smiling at me; he was waving good-bye. That moment is etched into my brain forever.

I roamed through the quiet streets of Dillingham as the hours stretched on. I returned to the airport early to wait for Stephen. I wasn't the only one waiting at the airport, though. There was an airport official quietly waiting for me. "I'm sorry, Inez," the official said as he met me at the door. "We've lost track of his airplane and Stephen hasn't returned."

I stared in this man in disbelief. Not my Stephen! I felt faint and sick, and the pain in my neck that had made me move so slowly all day long suddenly disappeared. "I don't understand," I gulped. "What do you mean, he hasn't returned?"

"I mean that we'll need to send a search-and-rescue team out if we don't hear from him. There's a bit of weather approaching and the area he was flying in will be fogged in. We can't do anything today. Go home. Wait for us to call you."

My eyes filled with tears as I stumbled back to the apartment. I poured a stiff drink and sat by the window. Numb and dizzy, I sat there for hours, waiting for the phone to ring. It never did. The next morning, when the sun's rays gave me hope that this had all been a bad dream, I called the airport.

"I'm sorry, Inez, but Stephen is still missing, and we'll have to wait for the fog to clear before we can search for him."

"Can I come with you?" I asked, somehow thinking that only I could find him.

When the fog cleared later that day, I joined the rescue team. Ten pilots were assigned to fly specific quadrants on the map where Stephen had been. We flew back and forth over white nothingness as I peered out of the window searching for a plane, a man, or parts. I could clearly see him stranded on a hill running toward us and waving at me once again. But that was only my imagination. It was not to be. Later that afternoon, another pilot discovered the burnt ruins of his plane.

Many years after the event, I finally understand that there is a reason for all that happens, although we may not see it at the time. My life had been spared and I moved on. I am grateful to Stephen for so many things. He taught me to appreciate the bigger things in life and to enjoy the moment. These days as I care for my two small children, I am able to enjoy them and see life through their eyes. In contrast to my own tense childhood, those days of love and freedom with Stephen taught me to relax with my own children and even to order room service once in a while. These are the days to treasure.

—Inez Caspi

The Apple Tree

I used to be a worrier when I was younger. Nothing was too small to capture my attention and divert my energies away from the things that truly count in life—things that we often do not appreciate until it is too late. As I teach in my seminars: At the end of your life, when you are rich in wisdom and have the big picture, you will realize that the things you now believe to be the big things were actually the little things. And the things that you now think are the little things are actually the big ones. Or, to quote Elisabeth Kübler-Ross: It is only when we truly know and understand that we have a limited time on earth and that we have no way of knowing when our time is up—that we will begin to live each day to the fullest, as if it were the only one we had.

While I was growing up, my father—who grew up near the Himalayas in India and was a man of much wisdom—once shared with me that the Sanskrit character for funeral pyre is strikingly similar to the Sanskrit character for worry. I was surprised to hear this and said so to my dad. His response: *You shouldn't be, Robin. One burns the dead, while the other burns the living.*

So about ten years ago, tired of spending my days mired in worry and lacking the energy to live the kind of life I knew I was meant to live, I decided to make changes in the way I conducted my life. To conquer the worry habit once and for all, I took up meditation, started practicing mantras, spent thirty minutes each day reading from wise literature, and began keeping a journal to record all the good things I had in my life (the elements I'd neglected to focus on). Within a matter of months I was much happier and more serene. I no longer worried about the fate of my career (I was a lawyer at the time). I no longer worried about the state of the economy or the health of the planet. I no longer worried about the rudeness of drivers on the freeways. I no longer worried about the length of the lines in the stores that I would visit. I even stopped worrying about death.

In particular, I began to see that human life is all about change. We are born, we grow, we learn, we die. Before this, the thought of a family member or a friend passing away was difficult for me to consider. But after cultivating a more enlightened perspective, I realized that whether we are here for a long time or a short one, every human life is a gift, and when a person is no longer with us, his life must be celebrated. I will give you an example.

At the health club where I exercise, I regularly encountered an elderly gentleman named Don. I never did learn his last name, but I was always struck by his decency, his warmth, and his generosity of spirit. You see, Don had a friend who owned an apple orchard. Every day that Don visited the gym, he would bring a grocery bag full of apples with him. After his workout, he would distribute the apples to anyone who was fortunate enough to be in the locker room. Over the course of the year that I knew Don, I came to know him as a man who never "sweated the small stuff." Every time I saw him, I received another apple.

One day as I brought my two children to the health club for a swim, the maintenance man stopped me in the locker room and asked me, "Did you hear about Don?" I told him I hadn't seen Don for a while. "Don died last week. His brain gave out and the car he was driving rolled off the road into a ditch. He was on his way up to his cottage."

Ordinarily, I would have been very upset by the loss of Don. But instead, I smiled as I fondly recalled all our conversations and all of his simple acts of kindness. Don may not have had his picture on the front pages of the newspapers, nor was he known to many. But through the size of his heart, he made more friends than he knew.

As a tribute to Don, a few weeks later my two children and I went into our backyard and performed a little ceremony marking the end of one life and the beginning of another. The three of us found a spot where the sun always shone, dug a little hole, and planted a seedling. My kids were pleased to see that our yard finally had what it had always missed: an apple tree.

—*Robin S. Sharma*

Less IS More

There I was, standing in my kitchen, smiling from behind my ironing board, iron in hand, ready to tackle the next shirt in the pile. With a snap, my life at that moment was captured on film.

I recently came across this picture, taken in early 1993. I was wearing my bright red "Sally Jessy Raphael" glasses, jeans, one of my husband's white T-shirts, and a blue plaid long-sleeved shirt. Pretty ordinary—until you notice my head.

I was bald as the proverbial cue ball, my head round and smooth, completely hairless. Behind me, taped to a kitchen cabinet, hung a computer sign stating in bold black letters, "Do it and get through it!" This was one of many signs with the same message hanging throughout my home. No room was left untouched by this message.

This was a time in my life in which I needed those signs. It was a time in my life when breast cancer came to visit, bringing along with it many unwanted "gifts." At first I opened its gifts of fear, dread, doubt, worry, and anxiety. Yet, as I traveled through the medical maze presented by breast cancer, I soon discovered new parts of me that had been sleeping in my soul, with no opportunity to present themselves until now.

Though breast cancer was definitely not the Welcome Wagon lady, it was a visitor who also delivered important gifts that stayed with me to this day: a newborn spirituality, newfound friendships, honesty, determination, faith, courage, and most of all, laughter.

Laughter was the one gift that literally helped me "do it and get through it." My sense of humor held steady through chemo, radiation, tests, visits to every medical "ologist" ever invented, and the unexpected complications. Even though I couldn't help wondering how soon it would be before my cancer returned, when I made light of my situation, laughing at the ways in which breast cancer turned my life around, somehow, on the level of the soul, I was shouting, "You may beat me, but not without a fight!"

I did laugh my way through breast cancer. It was my way of surviving. One day a hospital technician told me how much he enjoyed it when I came in for treatment.

"You know," he said, "most everyone who comes in here with cancer is dying. Maybe not in their bodies, but in their attitudes. You always come in with a smile, and you make my day a lot brighter." Little did he realize how much he was empowering me with that gift of words. It was what I needed to continue this journey with a smile on my face.

My radiation oncologist, Dr. Byrnes, was aptly named. Every Monday through Friday for eight weeks I had to lie on a table for about thirty minutes to "burn away" any cancer cells that might still be making a home within my body. By the end of the treatment, I had a permanent rectangular burn in the middle of my chest. Yet each day I went there, I enjoyed the company of the staff who treated me. I enjoy dry humor, and this group of people had a sense of humor drier than the Tucson climate. At the end of my treatment, I sent the staff a basket of fruit and candies with a note attached which stated, "Thank you for the hottest time I've had in my life!" Another light note to add to my cancer survival journal.

Looking at this picture brought back the memory of the night my husband Jerry shaved my head. On the morning of January 14, 1993, about one week after my first chemo treatment, when I got out of bed, I looked down and saw that much of my hair was still resting peacefully on my pillow. "So it begins," I thought. I knew I didn't want to go through a period of messy hair fallout, so I was determined to do a complete sweep of my dome.

Jerry was quite hesitant at first to participate in this project, the result of which would leave him with a woman who was no longer the same one he married. After I nagged him for two days, he finally agreed to do the deed, but he insisted on waiting until eleven-thirty that particular night. He needed a laugh from a rerun of *Cheers* to bolster his willingness to fulfill my request.

Once 11:30 P.M. came and went, I was in the bathroom, a towel wrapped around me, scissors and electric shaver in hand. I was going to control how breast cancer affected me. Breast cancer was not going to control me.

Slowly my husband lifted the electric razor to my scalp. Slowly he moved it back and forth over my head as the hair dropped onto my shoulders and the floor with the softness and quietness of snow. By the time he was finished, we were both smiling as we looked at my reflection in the mirror.

The first thought I had was how perfectly round my head was. My scalp was so white. I had never before had the opportunity to see my scalp . . . not that I would have chosen to go down this road. Gingerly I touched my fingers to the stubble that remained. It felt strange. *I* felt strange. My husband was relieved that project was now completed.

I purchased five different wigs. I told Jerry not to worry. After all, now he'd be going to bed with a different woman each night. Wouldn't that be exciting? He just groaned, knowing full well that one of me was more than enough to handle at any given time. I knew that in a few months my hair would grow back. I wasn't sure what its condition, color, or curliness would be, but at least I knew it was going to come back.

Even though I had purchased a variety of wigs and colorful, funky scarves and hats, I wasn't much for wigs or hats. The freedom and extra time I enjoyed because I had no daily or monthly "hair duties" liberated my spirit. Hair used to be a big thing for me. Often before when it was most important for me to look my best, I ended up with a very bad hair day. Leaving all of that behind was one gift from breast cancer that was a bonus. Eventually I went out au naturel, which brought comments and questions from strangers. Many people told me I had the perfect head for this type of "hairdo" and expressed the desire to be freed from daily hair care. Not one was willing to experience breast cancer to find out how they'd look, though, and I don't blame them.

One day we were visiting a garden center, and the resident artist, a sculptor, asked me if I was making a medical statement or a fashion statement. Smiling, I replied, "Well, I started out making a medical statement, but now I'm transforming it into a fashion statement."

The wigs, when I did wear them, must have appeared quite natural. While I was in the lab for some blood work, one of the secretaries exclaimed, "Mrs. Lenzo, your hair is growing in so beautifully! I love that hairstyle." She watched, stunned, as I pulled the wig from my head, handed it to her, and said, "You're welcome to borrow it any time!"

As I once again study the photo, I see that my chest is flat. A double mastectomy gave me balance. Whatever prostheses I might buy, my "breasts" would be the same size. I could even choose the size I wanted. Wow, I could be a bald Dolly Parton! What a sight that would be!

I don't wear the prostheses all the time, and I've been known to "leave home without them," which is fine with me. In the winter, they do provide extra warmth, but during the Tucson summers, which are famous for their heat, I enjoy the freedom of traveling sans "Dollies."

The prostheses cover my scars, which to me look like a pair of angel wings. I even thanked my surgeon for his artistic hand. Whenever I look down at my scars, which were later joined by a scar from the top of my breastbone downward toward my tummy, earned during a triple bypass a few years after my breast cancer surgery, I am reminded of a crucifix. My scars represent eternal life to me; they represent battles I have fought and won. They represent victory on a battlefield that produced real changes in my body, mind, and spirit.

Though breast cancer has left me with less body, I have received so much more because of the positive gifts it has given. This was one time in my life that less was definitely more.

—Fran Lenzo

The Big Move

Most would consider my first move rather insignificant, but for me it was a very big deal.

For over thirty years I lived on a 200-acre farm in northwestern Pennsylvania, twenty-five miles from Erie. My grandfather farmed the land and my father farmed the land, but the tradition ended with my parents' death six years before. My sister, a successful attorney, was happy practicing in Indiana. I remained in the farmhouse by myself while working as a communications specialist for a large regional insurance company in Erie.

I loved the farm—an emotion I inherited from my father. He'd sacrificed nearly everything to hold on to it. Unfortunately, I didn't have all the skills necessary to solve the problems that came along with the house, barn, and fields. The tough decision to sell came after a winter of frustration and heartache brought on by frozen water pipes, flying roof shingles, and costly snow removal.

I moved to the "big city" of Erie in September 1999. A few short months later, I was still living out of boxes in a cavernous apartment. The walls remained empty because I didn't seem to have anything big enough to make a significant statement on the antique white.

My commute went from nearly an hour driving at top speed in the dawn's early light to eight minutes of walking to my new office. It was easier, but I was having trouble calling my new apartment home.

I distinctly remember the phone call that caused the seed of the next adventure to sprout. It was a November night a few months after I moved to my new apartment. On the other end of the line was a friend from college, a nomad who just announced that his latest trek would take him from Boston to San Diego. "You should move there, too."

"Move to San Diego—that's a good one," I snorted to myself. I continued to half listen to him as I studied the bare walls of my apartment and eyed the lot number stickers still stuck on the sides of the furniture from my move in September.

With the phone pressed to my ear, I turned to the window and looked at the snow swirling down onto the dark pavement of State Street. Deep down inside me, something latched onto the idea. "Why not? You're practically packed as it is." That part of me already knew I wouldn't be staying long in Erie and, yes, I would move to San Diego.

A year later, I found myself onstage at my "good-bye and good luck" party at work. "This is as good as it gets—in Erie." I said this off the cuff (but into a microphone) at the party, and it became the quote I was most famous for among colleagues, family, and friends.

I quit a terrific job and tore myself away from a safety net of family and friends. My evenings had always been busy—my life in Erie was a blur of activity. And I would leave it all behind for a new beginning on the West Coast.

My friends were supportive, if more than a bit skeptical. "You landed a good job?" they asked. "No job," I said. "Do you know someone out there?" "I do have a friend from college, but he isn't the reason I'm moving." "Well, I'm sure you've thought long and hard about this."

"Oh yeah," I said. Not really, I thought. Because when I knew, I knew.

I had lived in the Erie area for over thirty years—plenty of time to grow roots—and yet I felt something pulling me away. A sense of adventure, maybe. The draw of sunnier skies, definitely. But something more that was undefinable and yet undeniable. Something inside that whispered, "Fly! Fly away! Let's see what you can do!"

It was one of those rare times when I decided to leap before I looked, and trusted that things would work out. To not sweat the small stuff in Erie or the big stuff in San Diego. To just trust and let go. And now it's as good as it gets—in San Diego.

—*Donna Kozik*

Thirteen Mornings with Plants

I stared at the clock on the classroom wall. It ticked loudly, the hands moving slowly, the red second hand sweeping around and around. For twenty long minutes I agonized over the ramifications of walking out of my computer science midterm. I was experiencing an extreme physiological reaction to the programs I was running. My temples were hot and throbbing, and the more I tried to take the exam, the more my brain rebelled and my synapses felt ready to snap. A conscientious student, I'd never dreamed that such a moment would ever happen. And this was a class I needed in order to graduate at the end of the semester. Walking out now would not only hurt me academically, it would hit me in the wallet.

Squeezing my eyes shut, I came to a decision. Closing my notebook, I placed it in my backpack and walked up to the professor. I handed him the exam and quietly told him, "I cannot do this. I have to drop the course."

He looked at me sternly and sincerely, folded his arms atop his bulging belly, and replied, "Are you sure?" I nodded and walked out.

First on my list was a stop at the local café. Perhaps a latte and a chocolate-covered graham cracker would quell my shame. I called a friend from the café and poured out my tale. He offered words of condolence, but I still felt like a failure.

The semester went on, and although I felt a tremendous weight lift after I dropped the course, I still felt the shame of giving up. My goal was to graduate from college before my thirty-third birthday, and dropping the course made that feat impossible. To make things worse, the ordeal added financial pressure at the worst possible time in my life. I was separated from my husband and no longer enjoyed the material comforts of a dual income. My options were to pay nearly a thousand dollars for a condensed intersession course in biology, math, or computer science that I could take during the four-week winter session, or to postpone my graduation and endure another whole semester and graduate in the summer of 2002.

I opted for the intersession course, not able to bear a wait of five more months for the gratification that I had been anticipating for nearly a decade. College was not just a coming-of-age ritual for me, as it is for so many young people; it meant far more than that. As I strode across that stage and accepted my diploma I would be the first person in my immediate family and the first on my mother's side of the family to acquire a college degree.

As luck would have it, the only class offered at the university during the intersession was the same class that I had dropped. Searching on-line at other universities for a course that my college would accept transfer credits from, I found a crash class in botany that the Biology Department chairwoman at my university would accept as a lab science course. One small drawback, though—it was offered at a university fifty miles away. Reluctant to do the commute, I signed up anyway.

"Thirteen Mornings with Plants" was the title on the syllabus. What a whimsical way to start! I had always loved trees and flowers, but never enough to study them for three hours a day, for thirteen mornings. As it happened, more than just the plants grew in those thirteen weeks. I did, too.

It turned out that the hour's drive to the other university allowed me to listen to National Public Radio, something I never really have the opportunity to do otherwise. Not only did I become more knowledgeable about world events, but I also learned how these events were affecting me. I used the ride home to ponder, which I love to do, and had some time to myself before going to work. Occasionally, I would listen to a book on tape, which was a great way to pass the time.

And the teacher! A quirky, wonderful biology professor with a Boston accent and a deep and eternal love for plants taught us interesting botany tidbits, such as the fact that eggplants, peppers, and tomatoes are really fruits, not vegetables; and that when we eat peaches, strawberries, and apples, we are actually devouring the ovary of the plant. Now I have a whole different appreciation of plants and vegetables. I have always been fascinated by trees, especially redwoods, but now I have a deeper understanding of their intricate workings, as well as those of other plants, which makes me question the origins of life more and makes me feel honored to share the planet with them.

Breaking my academic rules seemed like a shameful choice at the time, but that decision made it possible for me to have other rewarding experiences that I will never forget. Sure, I graduated one month later than my goal—just *after* my thirty-third birthday, rather than before it—but that fact makes absolutely no difference now. In fact, the delayed gratification actually enriched my life.

On the last day of class, there was no graduation ceremony, no cap and gown—just a real sense of pride that I finally did it. Like those of the plants I'd paused to study, my new roots took hold and helped me grow in a new direction.

—*Chris Bailey*

On the Road

"**L**ook out!" I want to yell every two seconds. Potholes the size of swimming pools. Children and donkeys veering on and off the shoulder. Construction detours that appear without warning. Huge trucks swaying with tipsy piles of sacks. Our bush taxi driver takes whatever Senegal's roads present him, wrestling calmly with the steering wheel. I picked this particular bush taxi in Dakar from among the many junky Peugeots because it has bright turquoise windshield wiper blades. They stood out like a hand-tinted detail in a black-and-white photo. A sign from the gods of road safety. That notion seems pretty ludicrous now as we swerve down the dry road.

I can't bear to keep watching what's in front of us. The trip takes four hours; I'd strangle to death on my stifled screams. Instead I focus on his Buddha-like expression, his firm hands. I try to adopt the Senegalese composure. They have a way of sitting apart even when crowded together, a dignified bearing that maintains them as individuals. Even in the middle seat, I'm barely aware of the passengers on either side. Around the steering wheel hang half a dozen necklaces bearing talismans, jujus, made of leather, shells, and twine—the West African version of a Saint Christopher medal, for warding off evil spirits. Faded and dusty, the same shade as the car, they have become part of it.

I fidget with the juju around my neck. Strung on its black cord is a small square chunk of black leather with a single white cowrie shell sewn on. A friend gave it to me, and I wear it almost constantly, a little extra insurance. You never know. My family back home is fretting about me traveling alone through Africa, with its crime, disease, and civil wars. I don't worry about those things so much as I worry about being in an accident in an overcrowded bus or rickety car.

But I'm also trying to understand in my bones how African days unroll, and I can't do that behind the wheel of a shiny rental car. So I focus on the passing scenery. Goats chew scrub and brush, while in the background, elegant mosques rise among thatched huts. Horse-drawn carts roll past stretches of garbage. Women and children carry sacks of rice, buckets of water, and baskets of fruit on their heads, swaying long-necked like giraffes. Our passing seems of no consequence.

I forget to wear my juju the day of the accident. Tamara, another person traveling alone, shares the cost of a ride to a bird park. We hire a taxi that's in tolerable condition—intact windshield and windows, four tires, no particularly loud clanking. The driver, Lamine, has "youth" written all over his animated face and twitchy body. I'd prefer an older, more experienced driver, but we want to get on our way. Tamara and I settle into the backseat, and I focus on her curly brown hair and laughing eyes as we swap travel stories. Soon we're at the turnoff from the main highway. Here two roads run parallel to each other. One is the old road, still usable; but we take the new road, on an elevated bed with a high, steep embankment. It has oddly sharp turns, like the remains of a viaduct over a vanished city. Lamine pulls over to pick up an older man whose car has broken down. Saar folds his long body into the front seat, fingers his prayer beads, and watches the road with a jaundiced eye. As we head into a ninety-degree curve, the sharpness of the turn sets off an alarm in my body. "Slow down!" Saar says. It's too late. We're heading over the right edge of the road. The tires are bad, the young driver overcorrects, jerking the wheel to the left—and we careen across the road, down the other side. Cursing aloud, I think that this might still work out if he holds on and rides it out.

But Lamine is trying to yank the car back onto the gravel road. Everything turns over. We roll down the embankment, metal clunking. My mouth makes sounds, but the speed sucks the words out. I cling to the idea that the rolling will stop, crazily look straight ahead while flying upside down. We rock to a halt. I see only black vinyl. Feeling my breath, I confirm with my body that I'm not dying. Then panic. I have no idea where anything is—the ground, my legs, the driver, or my friend.

"Tamara!" From somewhere beneath me, her voice. "I'm okay. Are you?" We call to the men and hear their voices in turn. The car has landed on its right side, and I am practically standing on top of

Tamara. We all scramble out the left window. Brushing off our clothes, we check each other out. Without seat belts, we flopped around as the car rolled. Tamara's shoulder is sore, and I have a bump on my head, but we're laughing, relieved. Saar hit his head on the roof and suffered a few cuts; his smile trembles and he praises Allah. Lamine has not a scratch, but he is angry and unapologetic. To him this is a catastrophe that has been visited upon him. The windshield is shattered from hitting the bush that stopped us from rolling further, and the car's bright yellow body lies bent and dented like an old tin pan. Behind it, the dull plain stretches unbroken.

Tamara and I take photos of each other in front of the wreck, posing in mock triumph. I wear the tired, sun-glazed smile of a hunter next to a slain lion. The accident freeze-frames into another adventure tale. "Well, we expected to be in an accident in Africa, so it's good that we got this over with," I say, repressing my disorientation. The moment echoes my larger dislocation from the familiar, the way that I grope through Africa, seeking solid ground. We get another taxi with an older driver, who takes us safely to the park on the old road.

I keep going because that's what I'm here to do. One night in Mali, I hit the wall. I spend five grueling hours in a baché, a mini-pickup truck that jams fifteen to eighteen people in the back. I crawl out of that one and cram into another one, to get to the smaller adjoining town where I'm staying. The night air stabs in through the wooden slats, and we huddle deep into our clothes. The baché sways and rattles as though in a cyclone. I peer out at the road; it has a steep gravel embankment like the one my taxi rolled down in Senegal.

"What the hell am I doing here? I could be at home, driving a Honda to a heated office. God, keep me safe, just this one last time, and I swear I'll leave Africa. Tomorrow." The baché stops dead. The driver and his assistant climb out and take turns banging the engine with a wrench. It starts again. The driver guns the engine as though he could outrun its death. Two more abrupt halts and banging confrontations follow. When we stall out the fourth time, I burst into laughter.

What makes me think I can control my journey through life by choosing turquoise wiper blades, older drivers, or better roads, or by owning a car? Such vanity. I understand now the calm that good drivers have. The only real certainty is in our awareness of each moment, opening up like the unbroken plain. Our only control is in how we react to whatever happens on those curves.

The driver and a few passengers push the baché off the road while the rest of us collect our things to take the last two kilometers on foot. No one tries to talk, but we hang loosely together, sharing flashlights, a walking congregation. I hum "Amazing Grace." My head clears. In the windbreak of trees, evening flows like a river. Stars are out by the millions, so bright they seem to breathe with us. I drape the image around my neck like a juju.

—*Lisa Schnellinger*

Just Like Sandra Day

Ope of every woman's biggest problems is time. There's never enough. Try as I might, I am still haunted by my "should" list. As a child of the seventies, I simply assumed I would have it all, so my personal "should" list is quite daunting.

Then came the first baby, and as every mother knows, she changed everything. Before she was born, I assumed I would take a three-month maternity leave, find good childcare, and go back to work, continuing to conquer the universe. It had certainly been done before.

My mother's death just before my daughter was born gave me quite a wake-up call, so I was pretty open to the idea of rewriting the script. But I had committed to be back at work in three months and I had bills to pay, so I really didn't feel like I had much choice.

The week before I went back to work, I mustered up the energy to hire a babysitter and take myself to the hairdresser. My roots had gotten to the point where it looked like I was going for some sort of punk rock effect. If I was going to reenter the workforce fat and still wearing maternity clothes, the least I could do for myself and anyone who looked at me was to have decent hair.

As I sat under the dryer waiting for the bleach to work wonders, I picked up a magazine. Thumbing through it, I happened to see an article about Sandra Day O'Connor. Now, the old me would have loved reading something about a successful, powerful woman like that. After all, I was planning on just as stellar a future for myself. But the new me almost didn't look at it, because for a fat woman in sweatpants who measures her life in the two-hour increments between nursings, it was just too depressing. But Sandra in her judge's robes still must have had some appeal for me, so read it I did.

I can't even remember what the gist of the article was; all I remember was that while I was reading it, I had a flash of insight. As the writer described the honorable judge's brilliant career, I realized that when she was my age, she was a housewife! Not an attorney, not a judge. A wife, a mother, a housewife.

It was in that instant that I realized that life can be long, and there was a lot of mine still ahead of me. I was thirty and my daughter was an infant. If I got off the fast track for ten years, I would still have twenty-five years or more left to make my mark in the business world. That was more than three times as long as I'd already put in. All of a sudden I was free. I didn't have to do it all now. One of the problems with my "should" list wasn't just what was on it, but my assumption that all of the "shoulds" had to be done simultaneously.

I had been looking at my life in terms of the grand plan, each thing I did built on the last. I thought I had to continue heading down the path I was on. I suddenly realized that instead of looking at it in terms of what I had to get done by which ages, I should look at it as what it was—a life, not a business plan. I didn't have to plan everything now.

And with that newfound wisdom (not to mention my newly done hair), I walked out of that beauty salon with a revised outlook on life. I still have a "should" list; of course I do. But I know that if I don't get around to doing it all, my life with my daughter will have been full and rewarding.

—*Lisa Earle McCleod*

A Look in the Mirror

The other day while putting on my makeup, I stopped and stared carefully at my face in the mirror. I remembered that when I was a little girl, I had a constant need to look at myself in the mirror, especially at night. While getting ready for bed, I'd fantasize about the glamorous life I really led—a life in which I was a television spokesperson for all manner of commercial products. In my fantasy, I sometimes sold toothpaste, smiling and posing and tossing my hair. Occasionally I'd branch out and try to sell shampoo or hair spray. Each night I'd spend an hour in front of the mirror talking to my invisible but admiring audience. Time was of no importance at that age, and living in the moment took precedence over anything else.

At thirty-nine, I've matured enough to know that if I talk to myself in the mirror, my husband might start looking up psychotherapists in the yellow pages. Instead, I quietly observe my face and think about the day ahead. Time is of the utmost importance, for I have little of it these days. Two young children often play at my feet. Several times in the past few years, I have run my finger along the subtle lines that have begun to appear on my face. Optimistically I tell myself that these are mostly laugh lines, not drawn from the effects of stress and worrying, but instead from laughing at jokes, life, and the antics of my children.

The mirror is the first "person" to see me in the morning. We have a great relationship. The mirror doesn't lie to me or tell me that I'm beautiful when I know I look tired, pale, and listless. But when I do look good? I swear, that mirror smiles back at me. It seems that mirror knows me better than I know myself. I've often leaned on the sink and gotten so close that my breath fogs the glass. What am I looking for? It seems I'm trying to see inside myself. What is my purpose? At this age, I ask myself that question frequently.

When I was younger, older folks would always tell me, "Time will go so quickly in your life. Enjoy yourself." It seemed I was too busy to ask what my purpose was or how I intended to fulfill it. A few years ago, I worked with a woman named Lorraine. One summer afternoon, she was notified that her mother had breast cancer and that it would have to be treated aggressively. The day after she heard the bad news, I stopped her in the hallway and tried to comfort her. She said to me, "I've learned one thing from all of this. You just never know when your time will come." The very next day, Lorraine herself was killed by a runaway truck while walking on the side of a road with her husband.

Maybe all of us can name at least one defining moment in our lives. Finding out about Lorraine's sudden death was one of mine.

Somehow I knew that Lorraine might have found her purpose in life just hours before she died. I was a confused twenty-three-year-old girl then, living in California with a boyfriend who wasn't committed to the future of the relationship. I was dreadfully homesick and worked at an unfulfilling job. Yet I stayed in the relationship and at the job because I was more afraid to leave than I was to remain. Lorraine's last words to me forced me to rethink the direction of my life. Shortly after Lorraine's death, I moved back to the Midwest to achieve my long-awaited goals, without my boyfriend.

I would imagine that most of the time we are unaware when we touch someone's life with words we consider unimportant, but which the recipient considers profound. When we confront the fact that we are entering the second half of our lives, we begin to ask ourselves serious questions. What have I done with my life? Have I achieved my career goals? Have I spent enough time with my family? What is most important to me personally? Am I too caught up in sweating over the small things in life? How do I achieve a balance between what makes me happy and what is best for my family? And all these questions are indeed important ones, but it is also important to realize that fame or fortune does not make a great life. What makes a life fulfilling is discovering how you have an impact on the lives of others in small ways each day. Instead, ask yourself, "Have I been a powerful force in someone else's life?"

The mirror doesn't lie. Each day you can find your purpose by looking in the mirror, reliving the moments you consider meaningful and inspirational, and cherishing those as the ones to remember. You never know who might have a defining moment in life simply because of your encouraging words or a story you've told. My life took an entirely different turn because of a casual comment from a woman who thought she was talking about her own mother's life but turned out to be commenting on her own death the very next day. While looking deep in the mirror for your own purpose, you may just help someone else find his or her purpose.

—*Vicky DeCoster*

The Gift

I love public speaking now, but I can assure you that this wasn't always the case. My childhood was not the happy-go-lucky young years so many adults look back on fondly. No, I was the tall, clumsy child whom the teachers always put in the last row. On the playground I was always the last one chosen for the second team. In fourth grade, my pediatrician discovered that I had very poor vision. What an amazing difference glasses made—finally I could see the blackboard in the classroom and the ball on the playground. Life after glasses was better, but my shy and awkward early years had already taken hold of my personality.

In college I majored in nursing. One of the requirements for graduation was a class in public speaking. Every semester I postponed taking that class, hoping that it might be dropped as a required course. But every six months, there it was again on the list of courses I still needed. I pleaded with my advisor, "I'll take anatomy, physiology, chemistry, microbiology, even an advanced zoology—but please, NOT public speaking." My advisor was not moved, and I finally signed up. I suffered through the class. Fortunately, the speech professor was merciful and I passed. As I left that classroom for the last time at the end of the semester, I was relieved to think that I would never have to speak in front of a group again.

My nursing career took me to New York, where I worked in a hospital and quickly advanced to an assistant nurse manager. Setting my sights on a master's in pediatric nursing, I started taking classes at New York University. After only a semester, I hit a major roadblock: In nursing graduate education, one needs to declare a functional minor, and the only options available at New York University were administration and education. Well, here I was again, faced with imagining myself in front of a room full of people. How could I ever get up in front of a class of thirty-plus students and deliver a lecture? Impossible. Education was clearly not a choice.

So what about administration? What if, as an administrator, I was called before a corporate board? Inconceivable! What was I to do? I did what any reasonable person would do—I fled. I left a city, job, and employer that I loved and all of my friends, and moved to a city where I knew no one so that I could find a college with more choices for a minor and avoid ever having to do public speaking.

And life was okay for a while. I got my master's, got married, moved to California, and started my family. I became active in my children's school, eventually becoming PTA president and chair of the legacy gift the year my oldest daughter started sixth grade. At the graduation ceremony, the president of the school board came to me and asked, "Does the PTA have anything to say to the graduates?"

My stomach flipped. My hands grew clammy. I looked anxiously at the crowd gathering and said, "Oh no! The PTA has nothing to say to the graduates." Then I turned to the friend sitting next to me and said, "Would you make the legacy presentation to the class? You speak so much better than I do." She said, "But, Marty, you did all the work." I said, "But you are a better speaker than I am, and I think it would be better for the graduates if you made the presentation."

My daughters were devastated. They felt that my friend had stolen *my* thunder—*their* thunder. I had taken from them the opportunity to feel proud. I had ruined my daughter's sixth grade graduation.

"This has got to stop," I thought to myself the next day as I hung up my daughter's graduation dress. "Never again will I make a major life decision based on fear." I was determined to get myself out of the box I'd lived in.

I enrolled in a self-improvement and public speaking class that summer. It was very hard, but I completed the class. After the class ended, though, I knew that I would once again revert to old habits unless I made myself speak in the front of a group on a regular basis. I'd heard about Toastmasters, the international speaking club, and found a club that met weekly in my area. Swallowing my fear, I joined up.

Was everything easy from then on? Did the pearls roll off my tongue as I stood at the head of that group? Not at all. In fact, I felt physically ill each week as I drove to the club meeting. It took me months to work up the courage to give my first speech, and I can still tell you the exact date on which I gave it—January 9, 1990. When I got up from my chair that day to give my four-to-six-minute "icebreaker" speech introducing myself to the club, I walked to the front of the room, turned to face my club members, and found I couldn't see anything but a white haze. As I gave my perfectly memorized speech, I was worrying, "How am I going to get back to my seat without falling down or bumping into someone?" Fortunately the room was configured with a head table and two side tables. I traced my hand along the backs of the chairs and found my seat. After half an hour, my vision started to return.

What kept me going? The memory of the pain in my daughters' voices when I'd ducked out on the PTA speech. I gave speech after speech in front of that Toastmasters club and even ran for a position in my district, which meant that I had to give a campaign speech in front of two hundred people. As I walked back to my seat afterward, I thought, "Hey, this is fun."

The best gift, however, waited for me when I got back to my seat. My younger daughter, Tammy, was sitting there, a huge smile on her face. She said, "You nailed it, Mom." The fear and guilt were gone. I was free.

—*Marty Taub*

Lost and Found

Only two days left. Two short days before I had to head home to California, and I still hadn't made my big decision. As I drove down Oregon's coast road, sunlight flashed off a sign advertising horses for rent. Ride a horse? Now that sounded like a fun break from driving. I hadn't ridden in twenty years, but I pulled into the stables.

The corral was filled with horses of all sizes and colors, but a chestnut roan named Aagor caught my eye. Standing tall and arrogant, he looked fresh and challenging, but strong and courageous. I felt an immediate connection to him as I hoisted myself into the saddle. Trailing behind three other horses, we plodded toward the shore.

Frothy white breakers smacked against a long silver beach stretching for several miles. The rush of the ocean was all I could hear. I shortened Aagor's reins and gently squeezed his sides. He tossed his head, reared up, then lunged forward, bolting like a racehorse on steroids. I was flying. I was free.

As we raced against the wind, chills ran down my spine as the weight of a thousand useless worries fell away. I suddenly understood. I dropped the reins against Aagor's neck, threw my arms in the air, tilted my face up to the sky, and whooped for the me I had lost... and found. Snorting through flared nostrils, the roan ducked his head and ran harder. When he finally stopped, flecked with sweat, I fell over his neck and hugged him hard, laughing. My mind was settled at last—I'd made my decision.

For the past ten years, my life had been good. I was a beach bum with a difference—I had a secure, well-paid job, a nice home, and a cute little dog. I zipped around town in a shiny silver sports car. I traveled several times a year, and on weekends sailed with friends around the harbor or lay on golden beaches acquiring a tan George Hamilton would envy. In the evenings I joined friends for dinner, went to the movies, or roasted marshmallows over bonfires at the lake.

At work, I was known as the creative one. It's funny, really, because banking is such a black-and-white industry, governed by strict compliance and stern and silent auditors. As a manager, I had a lot of responsibility. But I jumped at every opportunity to stretch and challenge myself, and over the years had carved a nice niche. At times I was too outspoken and driven, and thought too far outside the box for the comfort of my "superiors." For the most part, they left me alone because I did my job very well.

But as good as things seemed, my priorities began to change. I endured a painful separation, losing my best friend-partner-husband in one fell swoop. On the surface everything looked fine. Even close friends marveled at how quickly I recovered. But when I got home and closed the door behind me, I'd often curl up with my dog

Ben and cry myself to sleep. I felt trapped in a superficial life run according to everyone else's petty rules and expectations.

I started reading everything I could lay my hands on about self-empowerment. I delegated more of the business side of my job and helped develop some of the younger members of my team who showed a desire to learn. It was gratifying when I saw them promoted, moving on to new and exciting lives. But after a while I started feeling left behind.

When I lookd around for a new career to invigorate me, my uncle suggested his business—he was a stockbroker. With his help and encouragement I got my broker's license. All I needed now was to move from the world of banking to a brokerage house. What was stopping me?

While I dragged my feet about changing careers, I signed up at school to take an English refresher class. It was fun to be back in school, and it gave me something to focus on other than banking, brokering, or being newly single. Everything the typical student hated, I loved. Researching, writing, digging through archives— what could be better? I loved being surrounded by books, working on term papers until three in the morning. I was older than most of the other people in the class, but I loved learning from fellow students who were half my age.

By spring break, I'd interviewed with three major brokerage houses and received two offers. My head was spinning. I wanted to make the right decision, so I planned to weigh my options during a week's vacation in Oregon. Little did I know how one beach ride would impact my life.

As Aagor churned the sand, hooves pounding, I realized how hungry I was—for change, for new challenges. I could smell it. I could taste it. I could not continue at the bank. I could not become a broker. It meant letting down my uncle and disappointing others. But if I was going to take risks and make the kind of sacrifices needed for a successful career transition, then I must do what I really wanted to do.

And although I'd never said it out loud to myself—let alone to anyone else—what I really wanted to do was continue at school and make my living as a writer.

When I returned to California, I quit the bank. I traveled up the East Coast and down the West Coast visiting cities and universities, eventually deciding on Seattle, Washington. I knew no one there, but it felt right.

Four years have passed since my ride on the beach in Oregon. I keep a picture of Aagor and me on the wall in my writer's studio. It reminds me of the moment when I realized I was trapped in a prison of my own creation. When I knew without doubt that freedom is not just about having choices, it's about exercising those choices. It's about not sweating the small stuff and being true to yourself. Knowing who you are and what you want, and having the courage to follow your bliss. I'm still flying. And I'm still free.

—*Vicki-Anne St. Clair*

A Bucket of Seashells

Several years ago, while living in Southeast Asia, I went with a friend to visit a Buddhist monk at his pagoda in Vietnam. The monk was the brother of my friend's language teacher, and had been caring for the valley around the pagoda for several years.

That afternoon I found myself sitting in a chair on a small porch outside the hut he called his home. There was little inside the hut, just a sleeping mat of woven reeds and books, hundreds of books stacked neatly against the walls. The books were for study, the monk explained, but the valley was for living. The three of us sat outside the monk's home for some time that day. We were high above the valley surrounded by a rim of rock and nestled within a forest of tropical trees and plants. I could see out through the trees down to a plain that opened up below. There the Song Be River slowly meandered through thousands of rice fields dotting a dark, wide delta. Beyond were the waters of the South China Sea, and I knew that somewhere out there was home.

As we sat there that day, the monk talked. He told us about the young monks and nuns who had come to study with him, and he spoke of the valley he would protect until he died, simply because no one else would. He told us about the stories he'd written and the importance of finding one's way. Everything about that gentle man touched me and yet for him, this was just the way he was. Nothing more, nothing less.

As my friend and I prepared to leave at the end of the day, we asked the monk if we could return to the pagoda and perhaps spend a night there. The monk just smiled and replied that if in fact we did return, he would surely rejoice, for it would be good to see us again. But he also said that if we never returned and he never saw us again, he would rejoice as well, simply for the day we'd spent together.

I never went back to the pagoda, though I always wanted to. I left Asia a few months later and life got quite hectic after the visit with the monk. But I never forgot him. I never forgot his wisdom and his insight. I never forgot the way he was and the feeling of having been touched by something very good. I wanted to tell the monk all these things. I wanted to thank him and let him know that he had indeed touched me; that he had made a difference in my life and the way I viewed it. But mostly I wanted to tell the monk good-bye.

As the years passed, I struggled to find a way to explain the experience I'd had with the monk. Every time I tried to tell someone about him or write something wonderful about the day, I failed. No magic words could capture his being. How, I wondered, could I ever describe such a truly spiritual man? How could I ever share him with anyone else? And how would I ever remember him?

Then another friend of mine, a woman who has offered her wisdom to me for many years, told me something that seemed fitting. She said that as she'd gone through life, she'd collected memories of people and places like seashells on a beach. Whenever some beautiful memory came along, she would pick it up and put it in the bucket that was her heart. Later, when she had the time or the need, she would bring out her bucket and study the beautiful seashells she'd collected.

The monk, I realized, was just such a seashell. And when I looked into my bucket, I realized I'd collected many beautiful seashells throughout my life. Some of them were people and friends who had shone brightly in the bucket since I was very young. Each of the beautiful seashells in my bucket, I realized, was the memory of someone or something that had inspired me or touched me for a day or even just a moment.

The monk, I know, smiles at this. He has always known about the bucket. And while I have come to realize there are no good-byes, there are no ends to things, the monk just smiles, pleased that I finally understand.

I no longer feel the need to return to the valley high above the Song Be River to say good-bye. Instead, whenever I have the time or the need, I bring out my bucket and look at the beautiful seashells I've collected, and I know my monk is there.

—*Allison Pease*

Tears

We sat clustered together in my husband's hospital room, near his bed. Ron had been diagnosed with terminal lung cancer just two days before. Our family was clearly in unfamiliar territory, stepping carefully, each of us needing to find a way to travel this frightening new path.

Shannon, our Down's syndrome daughter, sat next to me, holding my hand, leaning against me, her head resting on my shoulder. Her visits with her dad needed to be kept short, as she has always disliked hospital visits of any kind. I don't believe her aversion is to hospitals themselves, but more to the fact that sick and hurting people are there, coupled with frustration at her inability to do anything about it. Shannon's love for others is a trademark of hers. For example, whenever one of her schoolmates was absent due to illness, Shannon cried. It was necessary to assure her the person was going to be okay in order to console her.

Shannon suddenly let go of my hand and stood and walked to the doorway. As she stepped out into the hallway, I saw her glance back over her shoulder. I saw tears coursing down her cheeks, and it hit me that she had been making sure she was out of her dad's line of vision before she let the tears come. It was heartbreaking that Shannon felt the need to hide her tears from him. It was not at all like her.

Adding to my heartache for my sweet daughter was the fact that although we had not shared with her the seriousness of her dad's condition, she obviously understood more than we would have thought. For Shannon, too, this was definitely uncharted territory. And she was even less prepared, even more helpless than the rest of us.

I went straight to her and held her, crying along with her. When we finally went back into the room, I gave the speech I needed to give, the theme of which needed to be shared with many others throughout the coming months. "Shannon went out in the hall to cry, because she didn't want Dad to see her tears. She doesn't have to do that, and neither do we. When something sad happens, people cry. Let's remember through this time, guys: when we feel like crying, we'll go right ahead and cry!"

It was true that each of us needed to find his or her own path through this painful period. But removing boulders collectively enabled us to begin the journey. I had known and loved Ron for thirty-two years. No one needed to assure me that he would agree with my "rule." Our eyes met, and he smiled at me. Seeing her dad smile, Shannon smiled, too, through her tears.

—Alison Peters

PART IV

DON'T SWEAT THE SMALL STUFF WITH CHILDREN AND FAMILY

Father's Day

The first time my one-year-old grabbed my leg as if I were the mast of a ship in the midst of a storm-tossed sea, I felt—well, frankly—omnipotent. However, when my little heroine clung to me in the same manner every time I tried to go use the bathroom, it was clear then who was really dealt the royal flush.

Kayla is my only child. She is also the first baby I ever held. Everything she does is new to me and just as new to her, too, I suppose. But today is Father's Day, so I'll stick to my side of the story out of respect for the moment.

In fact, at this moment, it's about 4:15 in the A.M., and I'm carrying Kayla in a baby carrier on my back as we ride an elevator down through a Montreal hotel. When we slip through the doors into the lobby, we startle the night clerk, but he is quick to realize we are no threat to him. Kayla, peering over my shoulder with wide eyes, and I, looking half asleep, hardly rate as a three-alarm fire.

"She's teething?" he asks. "Yeah." I nod. He gives me advice about a medication that he used with his kids that he swears is terrific. I wait expectantly for him to pull some from under the counter to help Kayla go back to sleep, but he never does. Instead, I ask him for paper and a pen and take up temporary residence in the mezzanine's telephone cubicle, where I can stand, sway, and write.

Boy, my baby's heavy. As I adjust the shoulder straps, Kayla reaches out for the phone. I wonder who she wants to call at this hour. I thumb through the yellow pages, giving her suggestions. "Perhaps a good psychiatrist to get to the root of this sleep disorder," I offer. "Or wait, let's see here, pizza, plastics, plumbers—yes, what about a plumber?" My ideas bore her, and she becomes quiet again.

If I had planned the perfect Father's Day with my daughter, I would not have chosen to begin quality time quite so early. Perhaps breakfast with Kayla's mom and Auntie Eva would have been a nice start. I imagine them both snuggled up in their beds in our room. Eva, who is seventeen, dreams of being at home with her friends, and April, my wife, plans our next vacation move in her sleep.

I can't help but wonder if Kayla will think well of me in, say, fifteen years for taking her on this trip to Canada, and then to meet her great-aunt and uncle and some of her cousins in Pennsylvania.

Or will this time together become just another roll-your-eyes-Yeah-right-Dad-whatever-you-say kind of memory to her? I can hear her future adolescent voice saying, "Dad, isn't there *anything* you didn't tape? Can we turn off the VCR now? I want to hang out with my friends." But those confrontations are far in the future, and I shouldn't spoil this moment by dwelling on them. Perhaps it's better to focus instead on the tiny sigh I just heard.

Warm wisps of breath occasionally caress the back of my neck. I can tell she's getting tired. I love it when she rests her head so softly on my shoulder. I like to lean my head back and use hers like a pillow. I wonder if she feels as warm and secure as I do when we are this way together. I close my eyes and sway back and forth in our cubicle, and I dream that, whatever storms my Kayla may face as she grows and learns about her new world, she can depend on me for refuge.

I feel the straps of the backpack tighten against me and I sense the familiar weight of a sleeping baby. Tired, and shoulders aching, I am grateful for the chance to be with her on Father's Day.

—*Samuel P. Clark*

The Secret of Successful Parenting...in One Word

In the fall of 1996, I was traveling across the country discussing my book, *How Good Do We Have to Be?*, which is about the sin of perfectionism and the guilt we feel when we discover we can't be perfect. In each city, I would speak at a local bookstore, be interviewed on local radio and television, and hear Protestants, Catholics, and Jews compete as to whose religious upbringing was more guilt-producing.

In one city, I had just completed an appearance on the noon news when the anchorwoman, an attractive young woman in her early thirties, took me aside and asked if she could ask a personal question. She started to describe problems she was having with her young children at home, problems with eating habits, getting them to bed, breaking up arguments. She said, "I don't know how much of it has to do with my being away from home so much because of my job, missing school plays and dance recitals. I try so hard to get it right, but nothing seems to work."

I told her, "This isn't the time or place to go into this in detail, so let me give you the short answer instead. The short answer is, RELAX! If your children know that you love them and that your love will not be arbitrarily withdrawn, they will survive your mistakes and imperfections. You'll be absent, you'll be cranky, you'll be distracted, you'll make mistakes in judgment, and none of that will do permanent damage. Get over this idea that thirty years from now, your daughter will be telling her therapist that she can't sustain a relationship because her mother didn't come to her dance recital. Your children don't need a perfect mother. That would be the worst thing you could do to them. That would make them feel inadequate when they grow up and learn they can't be perfect, which I suspect is what happened to you. And they especially don't need a mother who is tense and frantic all the time trying to do everything right. What your children need is a role model of how to say, 'I'm sorry, I was wrong, I'm doing my best and trying to learn from my mistakes.'"

The secret of successful parenting, I tried to tell her there in the hall of the television station, was contained in these few words: Relax and love your children. All sorts of good things will follow.

—*Rabbi Harold Kushner*

The Wake-up Call

As the telephone rang, I debated whether or not I should answer it. Struggling to get my two-year-old daughter Savannah down for her nap, I was not having the best of days. The day had started off on a positive note. After going to the studio to get Savannah's pictures, I was thrilled that her photos had turned out well.

Unlocking the door of our home, I was still thinking of those pictures. I was going to frame the large one for the hallway, and just could not wait until I could give the rest of the pictures of her as gifts for friends and family. However, when I turned around, those wonderful beautiful pictures had been crumpled in a tiny ball by Savannah's pudgy hands! I did not know whether to cry or be angry. That is when I decided that it was time to put Savannah down for her nap.

The phone continued to ring. Fearing that the call could be important, I decided to answer it. When I heard the voice of my good friend Sharon, I just could not wait to tell her my frustrations over Savannah's pictures.

After Sharon explained that she had called and missed us earlier, I informed her that we had gone to pick up Savannah's pictures. "But you will never guess what Savannah did!" I took a deep breath to continue my tale of woe, but she interrupted me.

"Speaking of pictures," she said, "my sister just called and said that she was going to get pictures of her two-year-old daughter taken tonight. She wanted one more picture of Laura before tomorrow."

"What is tomorrow?" I asked. Sharon's voice cracked with emotion as she told me that Laura had just been diagnosed with a tumor in her eye. Since the tumor was cancerous, her eye was to be removed in surgery tomorrow. Sharon's older daughter also had experienced this same health problem at the same age. Doctors had thought that was a fluke, but now, since Sharon was a nurse, she knew that this was no longer the case. The reality was that this terrible disease must be in their genes.

Sharon cried as she spoke of how she was reliving this terrible nightmare of a child losing an eye, as well as the ever-present fear that the cancer had spread. Knowing that her own two children could carry this gene to their children someday was almost more than she could bear. My heart was breaking for my dear friend. Sharon had been my inspiration to keep trying to have babies. Infertility, a miscarriage, and fertility treatments had discouraged me. But she stood by me. My heart hurt to see this pillar of strength being crumbled by her fears.

I listened as my heart was saying, "Thank you, Lord. I needed this wake-up call." My prayers began to focus on this terrible health problem instead of a bunch of silly pictures wrinkled (not destroyed) by the healthy hands of my daughter. The tears began to flow as I felt ashamed that I'd let this small thing become such a big deal.

"I am sorry to unload all of this on you, and for interrupting you earlier. What did Savannah do?" Sharon asked. My shoulders sagged. How could I tell her what I'd been upset about? "It really was nothing, and truly does not matter." I choked back a few tears. I sat in the kitchen for a moment after hanging up the receiver before walking upstairs to get Savannah ready for her nap. My child was only going into her crib, not to a hospital bed.

Her words of "Hold you, Mama," had never sounded sweeter, and earned her yet another story to be read. What was time? I sat in the rocker and Savannah climbed into my lap.

After only a few moments of rocking, Savannah fell asleep. Remembering Sharon's niece, I cried as I kissed both of her eyelids. I thanked God for all of my many blessings, including my daughter's good health and Sharon's call, which had reminded me of what truly does matter.

Savannah's picture now hangs in the hallway, wrinkles and all, to remind her mother not to get so wrapped up in a child's little imperfections that she forgets her many blessings.

— *Stephanie Ray Brown*

Luxurious Accommodations

It was just a question in passing. When a friend heard I was traveling to India, she asked, "Oh, are you going to Sai Baba's ashram?" I'd heard of this particular holy man, and I'd seen pictures of him in his orange robes with his halo of hair. So I said, "Sure. Where is it?"

It turned out to be in the tiny village of Puttaparthi, about three hours by taxi from the south Indian city of Bangalore. When our driver told my eight-year-old daughter Rachael and me that we'd arrived, I thought there was some mistake. There were throngs of people everywhere. We were supposed to be in a quiet Indian village; this was like Times Square on New Year's Eve.

"It's Swami's birthday," smiling devotees told us. I figured we could join the party; we had a room reserved, after all. "Room" is a curious word. In this case, it meant a three-by-five slab of concrete in a dormitory that might have comfortably accommodated 300 women. But this week, according to an Australian woman who had actually scored a cot, "I don't know, 6,000 maybe?" Perhaps.

"Rachael," I said, "Mommy's got to find our driver. We can't stay here. There's no bedding and we'd be sleeping on the floor with all those people."

"We can't leave." My sidekick paused for an instant. "We have to stay so we can know what it would be like in a homeless shelter."

I didn't have the heart to tell her that I didn't think a homeless shelter would have thousands of people bunking on concrete. Instead I said, "Okay, but just for the weekend." The Australian woman lent us a thin straw mat, which under the circumstances looked quite luxurious. Because there were too many people to accommodate at the canteen, and the village food was said to be unsafe for foreigners, we dined on a loaf of bread and two bottles of an Indian cola called Thumbs Up. Rachael and I shared our feast in the "tent" we rigged up from two scarves and a raincoat.

At three the next morning, we awakened to a swelling sound that started softly and built in power and intensity. It was the chanting of over a hundred thousand pilgrims gathered to celebrate. Waiting outside for dawn in the midst of chanting and prayers, I saw my little girl taking in the sights and sounds of this foreign land in a way that I knew was imprinting upon her soul. At that moment, a soft bed and a hot meal seemed pretty insignificant. I realized then that miracles don't necessarily come with the finest accommodations. And I was grateful that there are eight-year-olds in the world who know the small stuff when they see it.

— *Victoria Moran*

Some Things I Don't Know

1

"Mommy, can we see those dippers again?" my daughter asked as we pulled into the darkened driveway. We hadn't actually seen the dippers last time, but it didn't matter. This was one of those rare October nights when the air was still warm and the sky was clear black, sparkling with stars. Max and Katie clung to my hands. The leaves crunched under our feet as we made our way from the car to the house. "Where's the big one?" six-year-old Max asked, suddenly a scientist. He let go of my hand. Except for the outline of his head tipped back and the sound of our voices, there was only darkness. "Is that it?" he asked. "I don't know, I think it has one of the brighter stars in the handle. But I'm not sure." "I see it!" Katie called. "That floating one there!" "That's an airplane, Katie," Max said. "You can tell because it's moving. But if you see a falling star, that's a coyote falling to the earth."

"Did you make that up?" I asked, astonished. "No, a man came to our school. They told us stories. That one's from the American Indians."

What I don't know—about the stars and about my son and his distant school day. There are so many things I don't know. Once,

181

when he was smaller, Max asked me, "Is God up there?" "Yes," I said then. To me, up there was (still is) UP THERE, a place so vast, so infinite that I keep extending the edge in my mind until it dissolves away into forever. The kind of place, I thought confidently, where God would be.

"Where?" Max asked, wanting specifics. It is the vast broad spaces that catch his interest. But I don't know about up there or God. Some of the simplest things are hardest for me.

2

"I have a really hard question," the seven-year-old girl beside me called out. We were touring a nature preserve, part of a straggly birthday party group of children and parents. "How did God make himself?" Surprised, the tour guide, used to explaining the feeding habits of local birds, joked, "Wouldn't we all like to know that!" before turning away. She didn't see the look of disappointment on the little girl's face. But I did. I pulled her aside. "You asked the hardest question there is," I told her. "Even the grown-ups don't know." "You don't know?" she asked, awestruck. "Really?" Maybe she thought we were keeping it a secret, waiting for her to be grown-up, too, so we could finally reveal it to her with all the other mysteries of the universe. Later I overheard two four-year-olds talking as they stood on tiptoe at the ladies' room sink. "I know something," the first girl said. "Well," said the other girl. "I know something, too."

3

"It is not your job to know everything," my friend counseled. "If all you accomplish as a parent is teaching your kids to ask questions, to find the answers themselves, you have done everything you can." He was right, of course. But all along, like most of the people I know, I have been measuring myself and all the other people I meet by what I know and do not know. It's hard to tell the truth about not knowing, especially to my children, who depend on me to know everything there is to know, so they'll feel safe here on earth with me.

4

"Is a dipper like a stick?" Max asks. "No," I say. "It's more like a scoop." "Is that it? There?" "I don't know," I say. "I don't know." We huddle in front of the windows in Katie's room with the curtains draped over our heads, but all we can see are the headlights from oncoming cars, an airplane, our own reflections…

5

Katie thinks the moon follows us home. "I don't even have to look and I know it's there," she says. "So do I," I respond. I am learning from my children to have faith. Faith in the stars, in "up there," in what I don't know and probably never will.

6

"Mommy," Max said, "I don't think there's a Santa Claus." He was stirring flour in a blue and white bowl. I was pouring the water into it. "Why not?" I asked. "Craig's brother told me." "Do you believe him?" I asked. "Do you?" he returned, looking into my eyes.

Sometimes I marvel at the way children absorb guidance from every person, every stone, every star along the path. They take what they need from us and get the rest from others—grandparents, books, Craig's brother. But sometimes I wish that when they asked, I knew the answers. Which of those twinkling lights is supposed to be a dipper...where God is...when it is fair to reveal the secrets I know. "First do no harm," I remember someone saying once about something....So I say, "No, I don't believe Craig's brother." Then we slide the biscuits into the oven and wait for them to rise—like faith, like hope, like Santa Claus.

—*Amy Oscar*

A Piercing Inspiration

We all come to crossroads in our lives, but I was stuck at one for a long time until the light turned green.

I have always felt fortunate to be able to stay at home with my three children. So fortunate that I felt compelled to manage my family responsibilities, my volunteering obligations, and all housekeeping chores as seamlessly as possible. After all, this is what I did, and I thought I did it well. But at the point I had three teenagers, I was in perimenopause, and my husband was going through his own midlife crises. Add to this my new freelance writing job with a city paper, and our home life became somewhat unstable.

It was gradual decline, but since I had taught my family that I was the only one that did things correctly around the house, they never came to my rescue. Over and over again I heard, "Mom, my job is going to school; this stuff is your job," or "I'll do it later" (translation, "if I remember and I feel like it, I might do a slipshod job). I became indignant and the scenes got ugly, but despite my insistence, my family members only offered more resistance, I was a tired, resentful woman who felt everyone in the house should know what to do. The trouble was, they didn't—because I'd never taught them. This just wasn't working anymore.

I was determined to hang on to my new writing career, but I really missed the thorough way in which chores had been done all these years. I didn't want to be the maid or the concierge anymore, but my family had learned from me that they were incapable of clearing a table or making a hair appointment. Luckily, my fourteen-year-old daughter's insistence that she wanted to have her belly button pierced pushed me into a new realization: If I need help, I should ask it of the person who has the most to gain.

I know this sounds basic, but I had been doing it wrong all these years. I didn't know exactly how I felt about her request, but I did know I didn't have time to do the research on belly button piercing. So I asked Laura to do it herself and present the information to me. Admittedly, she was a bit taken back by this request, but since this felt more like a reasonable appeal than an order, she took on this job with a vengeance. Laura came back with an amazingly thorough report in just two days, and included both the good and the bad.

"Mom, did you know that your belly button doesn't heal for up to a year?" she asked, proudly waving her three-page report. Included with her point of view were the addresses and costs of the local piercing businesses, wound care and infection rates, as well as her plan to pay for the procedure and the jewelry. She decided that if I agreed to it, she would have the piercing done after the softball season, since her uniform might irritate it and cause an infection.

Truth be told, I was not very comfortable with the idea, but I tried to stay open. Laura said she understood that just because she produced the report did not mean that I was going to approve. But unexpectedly, after reading her report, I decided this was a harmless rite of passage that I could agree to if Laura promised to take care of it. I was glad that she felt protective enough of her body to postpone the piercing until after the softball season, and I complimented her on a sensible report and decision.

Believe me, this was progress. It eliminated hours of arguing and tears for all of us. I would like to think I would not have said things I would later regret, but I am amazed at how often I'd utter the same insensitive words that I'd heard as a child. Instead, I had guided my child toward learning that she could be responsible for her own favorable result.

I'm happy to say that after two months of softball, Laura lost her enthusiasm for a pierced belly button, and the whole issue was dropped.

I quickly applied the lesson I had learned to my children's other requests. You want the car, you wash it. You want friends to come over, then help clean the house. You want clean clothes, then get your clothes off your bedroom floor and into the laundry. It was a little late, but my kids finally understood that they were capable people with control over specific outcomes, and I learned to let myself off the hook.

When they were little, I *could* do it all, but I wasn't doing them or myself any favors, nor was I doing my job as a parent. I hadn't taught them to help themselves, nor did I realize this would become such a burden for me. Today I have let go of the small stuff like cleared-off countertops, dust-free cabinets, up-to-date photo albums, and a leafless lawn. In a family, it is about setting priorities, then letting go of unreal expectations. If this is how we teach, this is what our children will learn.

— *Mary Kate MacKenzie*

The Baby Box

While packing up my belongings to move to a new home, I came across a box in the back of the closet. Brushing the dust on it aside, I read the words "Baby Stuff." I hadn't seen this box in nearly four years, and excitement ran through me as I pulled the tape off. Inside this box were all the things I had saved from when my girls were babies.

The first thing I saw was a photo album. It was a small one, not much bigger than an average photo, but very thick. It was covered in the softest dark blue velvet and lined with silver trim. On the cover was a spot to place a precious photo or scrap of paper. What I placed there was the hospital card used to identify my firstborn. It was pink and white, with a pink teddy bear; it bore my last name, the room number, and the date Katherynn was born.

I opened the book and saw a photo of me lying on my side in the hospital, huge belly and all. The next few pictures were taken during my labor, and finally there was a picture of Katherynn as she came into the world. To a casual observer, the scene might seem gross. Babies aren't all pretty and clean when they're born, but to me she was a stunning vision, the most beautiful child in the world. The next photo was when they tried to take her from my arms; Katherynn grabbed my hair (which was quite long at that time) and wouldn't let go, her head tipped back and to the side trying to see me. We didn't break eye contact until she disappeared behind the nurse to get her first bath.

Another picture showed her first shampoo job, which she screamed through (to this very day she hates to have her hair washed). The book included Kitten's first-year photos (we started calling her Kitten right away): her first foods, walking and crawling, cute outfits, and new experiences.

In the middle of the book was another pink hospital card, this one indicating the birthday of my second daughter, Celeste. There was a series of similar pictures of her birth and the events surrounding it. I was taken back to that day, too. How she smelled, how she felt, how relieved I was to find she wasn't in danger at all. They had feared she wasn't going to make it, since her heartbeat dipped dangerously low for the hours I labored. All of us breathed a sigh of relief to find out she was simply squeezing the cord in her tiny hands with each contraction. To this day she has the same fierce personality.

I closed the book, held it to my chest, and felt emotions well up inside of me. In the box I saw baby clothes and old blankets. The sweet smell of babies filled the room and I could almost feel them in my arms again. I had saved several dresses and favorite sleepers, some booties and a pair of little pink leather baby shoes with Winnie-the-Pooh on the side. Both my girls had worn these. There were rubber bands holding tiny curls from first haircuts. "How different their hair looks now," I thought.

Clippings and photographs of family members and friends holding my babies, birth announcements and cards congratulating me on my new addition—all covered the bottom of the box. So many memories, so many items, so much love in those first years of life. I placed all the items back into the box, carefully folding and packing so nothing would be damaged. Everything was taped up inside except the blue velvet photo album. I kept that out for a reason. . . .

On days when I have had enough of the screaming, fighting kids, the dirty dishes and the stress, when I'm sweating both the big stuff and the small stuff, I close myself up in my bedroom and look at those photos. The pictures bring me back to reality. I may be angry with my headstrong girls and upset at the crazy things they try to pull, but when it comes down to the basics, these two will always be my babies. It takes me just a few glances at the pictures to remember how much I love them, and to refresh my attitude so I can deal with the ups and downs. Thank goodness I opened that box and found my treasures again. Sometimes we need that reminder of what it's all about.

—*Charity Stoops*

My Treat

I raised my hands above my head, lifted my eyes to the sky, and shouted, "What did I do to deserve this? Was I really that bad in a past life?" I lowered my arms and my eyes and glared at the round, flat slab of pizza dough at my feet. It was outlined by red spikes of tomato sauce, and looked like something out of a Stephen King novel.

It had been an extremely bad day. Work was more stressful than usual, and the babysitter quit because of something my oldest daughter said to her daughter. I tried to end the day by treating my daughters to homemade pizza, but instead fed supper to the floor.

"Mommy, did you say something?" My oldest daughter peeked around the corner. Sam was seven going on twenty. Her serious blue eyes looked at me, looked at the floor, then back at me. "What happened? Why did you drop the pizza on the floor?" My first impulse was to tell her that I wanted to. I did it because I just didn't have enough stress in my life and needed more.

"It was an accident," I said through gritted teeth. My throat constricted as I tried to hold my anger at bay. I was angry at Sam for asking what I thought to be a dumb question. I was angry at the babysitter for being so petty, and angry with my boss for having unrealistic expectations. But most of all I was angry with myself. "Oh" was all she said.

The room became terribly quiet. The only sound was my four-year-old daughter coming down the hall. Maggie skipped into the kitchen, oblivious to anything wrong. She stopped at my side, stretched out her arms, and asked to be picked up. I grudgingly complied. After giving me a huge hug, she looked down and saw the mess on the floor. "Is that our supper? Why is supper on the floor, Mommy? Can we eat now? I'm hungry."

I could feel my anger grow with every question Maggie asked. Then I looked into her innocent blue eyes. Her only worry was her hunger. A hunger that was nothing more than her internal clock telling her it was time to eat. I looked at Sam again. She stood there quietly and waited to see what I would do next.

I hated the seriousness and the worry I saw in her eyes. It was not my daughters' fault that my employer was unreasonable. It was not their fault that the babysitter got angry, and it was not their fault that their father and I had separated. Life as a single mother consisted of trying to juggle performing a full-time job, running a household, and raising two young daughters. I was tired. I looked down at our supper on the floor and sighed. It was definitely not their fault that I dropped the pizza on the floor.

I felt Maggie's little arms hug me tighter. "It's all right, Mommy. Maybe we can pick it up and wash it." I didn't realize Sam had left the room until I saw her come back in. She walked up to me and held out her hand. In it was a crisp twenty-dollar bill. "Don't feel bad, Mommy. We can buy a pizza." It was the money she had gotten for her birthday.

Tears welled up in my eyes and rolled down my cheeks. I knelt down and hugged her hard with my free arm. I felt the warmth of my daughters. Maggie clung to my neck on one side and Sam hugged me tight in the other, still clutching the twenty-dollar bill. The day's burdens lifted.

I realized that my employer would probably still be unreasonable tomorrow, but he could be dealt with tomorrow; my babysitter could change her mind about taking care of the children or I could find another one. And as for the pizza . . . the girls and I cleaned up the mess and I ordered a pizza for delivery—my treat.

—*Pam McInnes*

Small Packages

For what seemed like an eternity, I was ready to be a wife and mother. I have always felt that it was my natural calling, the reason I was here. I felt in my realm when I was babysitting or doing chores growing up. I think I began to save things for my hope chest in eighth grade. It was the one thing in my life that I was confident about: I knew I would be a good, loving wife and a wonderful, nurturing mother. I'd had such wonderful role models with my parents. My sister and I were my mom's career, and my folks have been happily married for thirty-one years now.

A few years after my husband and I were married, we found ourselves expecting our first baby. We were very excited about starting a family, although being away from friends and family would make it a little tougher, but we had each other for moral support. We read everything we could get our hands on and even watched the growth of the baby on an internet site that provided information about each week's development. For the first time in my life, I was ahead of the game, and so looked forward to staying home and growing with my new baby.

I remember clearly the day that all changed. It's hard to forget those precise moments in time when your whole world gets turned around in a single moment. We arrived at the doctor's office bright and early and full of water. I was five months into my pregnancy, and we were there for my first ultrasound. I'd been told that the more water I drank, the better the view we would have of the baby. I wanted to be sure to find out the baby's sex. I drank ten glasses of water and a couple of sips of cola. Yes, I listened to every ounce of advice to make sure the baby moved around a lot, for a better view.

I was ready to explode when they finally called me in. As I lay on the table, my heart thumping, the ultrasound technician put the cream on my tummy and my husband held my hand tightly. We were finally going to "meet" our little creation. This tiny person we had been reading, talking, and singing to every hour since we saw the two pink lines on the pregnancy test.

Except for the constant whooshing sound that filled the air, there was an uncomfortable silence. Why wasn't she saying anything? Finally, in a calm and even tone the technician asked if I was on any medication during my pregnancy. My mind raced. My heart sank. Why was she asking about medication? Did she see something abnormal on the screen? A whole catalog of possibilities went through my mind—a missing arm or leg. "What's wrong with my baby?" I demanded. Then she said the words that to this day echo in my thoughts. "Sweetie, there's nothing wrong. It's just that, well, there's two of them."

Never have my eyes filled with tears so quickly, my thoughts raced so frantically. "My God," I looked at my husband, "what are we going to do?" Ryan looked at me, smiling from ear to ear, and said, "We're going to have twins!"

Everything changed then. I had to go to a specialist for multiple pregnancies, as well as my regular ob/gyn. We had to get into our Lamaze class ASAP, just in case.

And the doctors told me that I needed to forget all of the information about pregnancy I'd been given thus far and forget all of the books I had read. I was now considered a high-risk pregnancy, not just an average pregnant woman, as I was before I had the ultrasound. I felt so unprepared. All of my self-confidence flew out the window. For the first time in my life, I'd thought I was ahead of the game. I'd read all the books and was ready to just enjoy the rest of my pregnancy. Now instead of just worrying about one baby, I had to worry about both of them. Will they have all the things they need to be healthy?

I sat outside by the pool that day and listened to the waterfall. I cried. "I am going to have twin daughters," I thought to myself over and over. The tears came from so many mixed emotions. Excitement over this incredible miracle. One baby is miracle enough, but *two*—that is just a phenomenon. And they are inside me! And there was fear, real fear of the unknown. So many things ran through my head. How on earth was I going to be able to do this? Just a trip to the grocery store or a walk, everything that I believed I would enjoy about motherhood, was now going to be more like a production line.

And I just could not help but feel, well, stupid. How could I not have known that there was this whole other person inside me? If I heard the phrase "God never gives you more than you can handle" one more time, I was going to hurt somebody. Ryan and I live 1,300 miles away from family and friends. I had always been confident about my abilities when it came to motherhood. But how did God expect me to be two mommies? I felt so bad for these innocent little babies. When they are both crying, which do I pick up first? Each baby needs a whole mommy to care for her. Could there possibly be enough of me to tend to both of their needs?

We didn't talk for a while, the Man Upstairs and me. Even now we have our days. But as time passes, I look back on all of the things Ryan and I have accomplished with the girls. They are so happy and full of love and wonder. I think back to the diaper changing and the breastfeeding which, yes, I did successfully for over two years. People always ask me, "How do you do it? I can't imagine two." And my reply is, "I'm not sure, I just do, and I can't imagine having only one!"

Ryan and I handle it together. We are a team. That is when I had an epiphany. God gave me the chance to exceed even my own expectations of myself. What it really came down to was not how difficult things would be, but how exciting our lives would become. Having twins is an experience that only a chosen few can have. As soon as I let go of all my expectations, as I decided not to sweat over the details but just to enjoy these little lives given to me, everything began to flow. Well, I got my girls, and I still cannot believe there are two of them. But every day I thank Him that there are, because I can't imagine my life any other way!

—*Shannon Pelletier-Swanson*

Cory

My seventeen-year-old son Cory was fatally injured in a lawn mower accident on July 20, 2000. Cory had so many plans ahead of him. It was his senior year in high school. He had already started making plans for college, and he was looking forward to what the future held for him. He was working with his father in his father's commercial lawn business when the accident happened. As you would expect, we were all completely devastated by this tragedy. Cory had just had his senior pictures taken the week before he died—he never even got to see them. He had his whole life ahead of him, but for some reason we will never know, Cory was taken from us.

Cory's father and I were divorced when Cory was a baby. He has an older brother, Eric. We are a very close family, even though their father and I had divorced so long ago. It was as if Cory and Eric had two complete sets of parents, and it was important to all of us that the children had a good life and did not suffer because of our decision to divorce.

Cory was a leader—at school, at home, or wherever he happened to be—and had his head straight. One day during the summer prior to Cory's accident, he and I had a serious conversation. He was concerned about his dad. Cory thought his dad worried too much. His exact words to me were "Mom, I wish Dad wouldn't sweat the small stuff—life's too short." Cory had embraced the "don't sweat" philosophy, and it showed in the way he lived his life.

At Cory's funeral there were over five hundred people—youngsters, older people, family members, friends, schoolmates, and some folks who didn't even know Cory, yet felt they should be there. There were so many attendees, in fact, that not everyone could get into the church. One of my dear friends stood before this large group and read on my behalf what I had written about Cory:

One of the most important things Cory taught me was "Don't sweat the small stuff—life's too short." He talked to me about that very thing just a few weeks before he died, and I know that powerful phrase had great meaning for him.

After this story became a part of Cory's funeral, this phrase became synonymous with the mention of Cory's name. The seniors at his high school had T-shirts made with Cory's picture on the front and *Don't Sweat the Small Stuff—Life's Too Short* on the back. It became the senior motto. We now hold an annual golf tournament called "Christopher Cory Soles Don't Sweat the Small Stuff Memorial Golf Tournament," which has so far raised over $15,000 in college scholarships for high school seniors.

At what would have been Cory's graduation, I ordered copies of *The Don't Sweat the Small Stuff Treasury—Special Edition for Graduates* to give to all of his classmates. The basketball team retired his number—33—and in the gym a big sign hangs under the scoreboard in honor of Cory. What does the sign say? What else? *Don't Sweat the Small Stuff*.

Cory's death has had an incredible impact on our lives, and it affected his friends deeply as well. He was a true inspiration, touching the lives of so many in his short seventeen years. By his death, he taught a lot of people what is truly important in life. He is sadly missed every day. Recently we had Cory's grave marker made and installed. At the very top of his headstone, it reads: Don't Sweat the Small Stuff!

I can honestly say that phrase has now become a statement used every day by my family and friends. We all realize that life is definitely too short to sweat the small stuff, and we don't. Cory, thank you for teaching us what is really important in life, and thank you for the wonderful memories you left us with. We love you, buddy!

—Debbie Smith

Christmas Still Comes

O n the first day of Christmas, there was no partridge in our pear tree. Instead, our dead tree was leaning precariously in the stand full of water it had long since stopped drinking. The angel had toppled as the tree began its forward tilt and our toddler, having her own idea of spreading holiday cheer, scattered ornaments all over the house. I started to wonder what the next eleven days of Christmas had in store.

Christmas has always been a big occasion for me. It could be said that I'm something of a Christmas nut because of how I immerse myself in the festivities: the tree, decorations, cookies, music, movies, even clothes—I just can't get enough. Over the years, I've moved steadily toward my dream of decorating every room of the house for Christmas, including the bathrooms. Decorating begins Thanksgiving weekend. Those in my neighborhood have an unofficial contest to see who can get their house lights up first. Christmas may be just a one day on the calendar, but for me, it becomes a way of life for six weeks a year.

Be that as it may, my daughter proved that she had no intention of cooperating with my holiday plans. I soon realized that her commitment to *un*decorating the tree was much stronger than my commitment to hold on to tradition. Out of frustration, I decided to give up fighting the losing battle and instead put my little darling to work. The next time she grabbed an ornament, I asked her to hand it to me and then encouraged her to bring me some more. By evening, the fallen angel, garland, and ornaments were all packed away.

On the second day of Christmas, I removed the lights and chopped up the tree. Branch by branch, it was soon ready for kindling. For me, this would be the first year without a tree on Christmas Day. This evoked in me an odd mixture of pain and indifference. True, it is lovely to awaken Christmas morning to a brightly lit tree surrounded by pretty packages, but hey, I was already tired of being poked by the pine needles that kept getting stuck in my socks. Why sweat the small stuff at this time of year?

So as tradition found its way to the woodpile, reality set in. Christmas does still come, even without a tree. I fondly recalled Dr. Seuss's *How the Grinch Stole Christmas*. As the Whos in Whoville gathered around an empty space where their beloved tree once stood and sang "Welcome Christmas," the Grinch marveled that Christmas had arrived even without the usual trimmings.

That's something we'd all do well to keep in mind. Christmas is not about the decorations around the home, but about having a place to call home. It's not about the food, but about being thankful for having something to eat. It's not about buying gifts for people, but about having those people in our lives.

By laying waste to the tree, my toddler had inadvertently reminded me about the true meaning of Christmas. So on the twelfth day of Christmas, when we built our fire in the hearth, we gave new meaning to gathering around the glow of the Christmas tree. Welcome, Christmas!

—*Peggy Sakagawa*

Mama Said There'd
Be Days Like This

People often tell me they're jealous of my life. I'm a freelance writer and a stay-at-home mom. I love my work. I have a terrific husband and four beautiful daughters, but what people don't see is the utter chaos in my home. There's never a dull moment around here!

One Saturday I got up early because I had a deadline to meet. I hadn't been able to get much done because of various distractions. Oh, heck, I'll just say it. My home was like a war zone. This particular day was one of those days when I just wanted to scream, and then . . . I did. It started when I heard, "I'm telling!" I hear this frequently, so I wasn't too worried until I heard, "That was Mom's good jacket." This got my attention.

It looked as if my jacket had been in a fight with a bottle of glue and lost. My industrious six-year-old tried to make me a surprise. She didn't mean to mess up my jacket. I told her to stop crying. I would find a way to get rid of the glue, and then I'd have a helpful hint to send in to one of those house and home magazines. Yeah, right. That and thirty bucks would get me a new jacket. I suddenly realized my baby had wandered out of the room. As I ran into the bathroom looking for her, my smiling toddler threw her slippers in the toilet. She giggled happily, but I was not amused.

I stomped over to the toilet, retrieved the slippers, and threw them into the washer. I washed my hands, brought the baby out, and made sure the bathroom door was closed this time. I went back to my desk. I had typed maybe two lines when my hormonally challenged preteen daughter approached me, looking very unhappy. Her favorite shirt wasn't clean. I guess she forgot I had to wash the baby's slippers first. Apparently this was not a very good excuse, because she informed me that I never did *anything* for her. She never got anything *she* wanted, but everyone else did. She stormed out of the room.

I started to go after her, but there was another commotion by the bathroom. The baby was still playing by my desk, so I was reasonably sure nothing else had been baptized in the toilet. I went to investigate and found my nine-year-old locked inside the bathroom. She refused to open the door or tell me what was wrong. When I threatened to unscrew the hinges and take the door down, she finally opened up. Her face was covered with blood! So was the sink. She had decided to pull a loose tooth, but obviously the tooth had other ideas.

By this time, I was getting tense. I doctored up my bleeding child, and as I was cleaning the sink, the phone rang. I could hardly wait to see what was in store for me next.

It was my husband calling to tell me he forgot his wallet. I had to load up the kids and bring it to him. I tried to convince myself that it was no big deal; I'd find time to write later. Somehow I wasn't convinced. I located my husband and handed over his wallet. Rather than thank me for coming down, he proceeded to tell me that it was my fault he forgot it because I was the one who moved it. Humph! I jumped in the car and slammed the door.

The slamming door woke up the baby. My older girls entertained themselves by fighting all the way home. They were yelling, the baby was crying, and by this point I was cursing under my breath. When we pulled up, I didn't even wait until they were out of the car. I simply yelled: "Go in your rooms and find something quiet to do or else!" I deposited the baby in her playpen and swore that I was going to get some work done at last.

I sat down at the computer and checked my e-mail first, hoping that perhaps someone had passed on a joke or two, something to liven up my now-black mood. Instead, I found a message from a dear friend of mine. Her baby, just two days younger than mine, had been diagnosed with a form of congenital heart disease.

Slumping over my keyboard, I ran my mind over the events of the day. I was ashamed of the way I had treated my children.

Instead of appreciating them and being thankful for their good health, I had been angry with them most of the day.

What reason did I have for being so upset? They were basically just being kids. They hadn't done anything really terrible or dangerous. They weren't ill or seriously injured. I should be thanking my lucky stars that the worst thing I had to deal with was a bleeding tooth or slippers in the toilet.

As tears streamed down my face, I sent off a note of support for my friend, turned off my computer, and left my office to gather the girls around me. They wondered why I was crying. I kissed them and held them for a long time, gently reassuring them of my love.

My friend's baby came through her procedure just fine. She is doing great now, but life sure has a way of changing our priorities. Sometimes it even teaches us a lesson through someone else's pain. I'm learning to appreciate my time with my family, even those days that test my sanity. Working is very important, but it's a little lower on my list now. My writing will keep for another hour or even another day. There's no guarantee that my family will!

—Sherry Holetzky

This Moment

As was our custom, I arrived at my daughter's school to take her out for our usual Tuesday afternoon together. The bell rang, and I soon spotted Haley with her radiant smile walking briskly down the hallway toward me. We joined in an embrace that brought the joy, warmth, and love that only a seven-year-old girl can bring her daddy. As we proceeded out of the school, she let out an electrifying shout: "Freeeeeee! at last." She grabbed my hand and we ran toward the car. Although the school disappeared in our rearview mirror, my lesson was only just beginning.

Our discussion turned to the day's plans. "What would you like to do today, sweetie?" I asked. "Well, Dad," she began, "it's getting colder and the ducks at the park probably don't have as much food now. How about we get some bread and go feed them?"

"Great idea," I replied. After a quick trip to the grocery store for bread, we were off to the park for an afternoon of fun.

As we drove along, my thoughts drifted from one thing to the next. I thought about my job and how unhappy I was with it. I wondered about that silly hesitation I kept noticing in my car. I remembered a disagreement I'd had a few days earlier and wondered if I had said the wrong thing. Dark thoughts about the "slowpoke" in front of me filled my mind. And of course, as is my usual custom, I worried about the tall stack of bills compared to the short stack of money. As we entered the park, my attention shifted back to the present moment. "Yay, we're here!" shouted my bubbly little backseat bundle of energy.

I sat on the bench watching her as she broke off pieces of bread and threw them into the pond. The resident ducks crowded around her and awaited her next offering. My thoughts drifted once again. It was like a tape recorder I kept playing over and over in my head. "I shouldn't have said that, he is my friend after all . . . what other job could I do . . . I hate my job . . . I need to earn more money . . . which bills should I pay first . . . should I get my car looked at?" This constant internal noise continued for several minutes.

My chatter was silenced by a strange voice. "She's beautiful," an elderly gentleman stated as he sat down on the bench beside me. I turned to look into his eyes, which seemed to overflow with joy, wisdom, and compassion. "Thank you," I replied. "That's my daughter Haley, and my name is Michael." "Nice to meet you, Michael. My friends call me Sam." Sam and I made small talk for a short while until Haley came over to us for more bread. I introduced the two of them. Haley smiled, said hello, and was off again to feed the ducks.

Our conversation resumed. "Interesting creatures, aren't they," said Sam. "The ducks?" I asked. "No, children. Children are interesting creatures. Take your daughter, for example. What do you suppose she's thinking about right now? Is she thinking about the homework she has to do or what time she has to wake up in the morning or the test she has on Thursday? Nope, none of that. All she's thinking about are those ducks and feeding them. Look how she laughs as the ducks climb over one another to get the bread. See how she threw the piece of bread to that one duck off by itself? Nothing else matters to her except those ducks."

As if reading my mind, he continued. "And here you are, letting the thoughts of yesterday and tomorrow steal away the only time you have, which is right now. That's all you have, Michael . . . this moment. You can't do anything about yesterday, and tomorrow is out of reach. It won't be very long before that little beauty of yours is off on her own, feeding her own children instead of these ducks. Enjoy this moment because it's perfect just the way it is." Sam casually said good-bye and left as quietly as he'd arrived.

As I sat there, his words hit me like a freight train. "That's all you have, Michael . . . this moment. Enjoy this moment because it's perfect just the way it is." I suddenly noticed Haley's unbridled laughter, the beauty of the trees, the warmth of the sun, and the ultimate perfection of "this moment." The chatter was silenced, and my heart was filled with the beauty that lay all around me.

I looked at Haley, and she ran toward me. She grabbed my hand, pulling me off the bench. "C'mon, Dad, help me feed the ducks! Isn't that why we came here?" Hand in hand, we ran back to the edge of the pond. We spent the rest of the afternoon feeding the ducks, swinging on the swings, laughing and playing. And just as Sam had so wisely pointed out, each moment was perfect.

—*Michael D. Pollack*

A Wedding in a Week?

Next to building a house, planning a wedding has to be the most stressful event in a person's life—especially for the mother in charge of the arrangements. As the master of perfection and worry, I was amazed at how calm I was when my oldest son announced that he and his fiancé had decided on a church wedding. That may not seem like a big deal to someone who has six months to a year to plan one, but what if you have only five days to pull it off?

As college students, Casey and Tina did not have much time or money to spend planning and paying for a wedding ceremony. While they were home for the Christmas holidays, the couple had their blood tests done and obtained their marriage license; they had planned to go to a justice of the peace upon their return to college. The two left on a Saturday afternoon, promising to inform us when they decided to tie the knot.

On Monday evening, my son called. "Mom," he said, "Tina and I have decided we want a church wedding." Thinking that they were postponing the event for a while, I said, "Whatever you decide is fine with me. I just want you to be happy."

"Do you think you can help us with the wedding plans?" "Sure," I replied. "Have you set a date?"

"This Saturday." "This Saturday?" I said, glancing at the calendar. "You mean January 13?" "Yes," he replied happily. Sensing some hesitancy on the line he asked, "Is that a problem?"

"Where do you plan to have the ceremony?" I asked, trying to recall every stress-reduction technique I'd ever used. After all, my firstborn was getting married. I was excited. "I was hoping you would call Reverend Smith to see if he could marry us at his church in Chelsea," he said. "Are you *sure* it has to be this Saturday?" I asked.

Knowing the demanding schedule of a vet student, I was not surprised when Casey replied, "Mom, this is the only weekend Tina will have free for about three months. We don't want to wait that long. Can you help us?" he pleaded.

"How many people do you plan to invite?" I asked, dreading his answer.

"Just the immediate family. We don't want a big deal made out of this, and we don't want you to go to a lot of trouble, Mom."

I asked some more questions about normal things: what they planned to wear, who they had asked to attend them, and what they had in mind for a reception. Normal things. I am a freelance photographer, so at least I didn't have to worry about hiring someone to shoot photos. One less obstacle.

Because it was such short notice, we didn't send out invitations; thanks to Alexander Graham Bell's wonderful invention we called relatives, who were as surprised as I had been when they learned of the upcoming ceremony.

There was, however, one small glitch in the plans. I talked to the Reverend Smith on Tuesday evening. He agreed to the plans, but could not perform the ceremony until seven P.M. Saturday. He said, "If they can wait until the next weekend, I can perform the ceremony whenever they want."

I told him I would get back to him after I talked to the couple. I did not know, however, that the minister was leaving town and wouldn't return until Thursday evening. I didn't know whether to continue making plans, like ordering a cake and a bridal bouquet. I decided to wait. A bit of a heart-stopper, don't you think?

After confirming the final arrangements with the minister on Thursday evening, I made a list of everything left to do. Our rural town's population is around 2,200. Ordering a wedding cake the day before the ceremony is really not a big deal. Neither is ordering a bouquet from one of the three local florists.

My future daughter-in-law, who does not have many occasions to dress up, had opted to wear a nice pantsuit for the ceremony. However, Friday evening—the night before the wedding—I received a phone call from my son who informed me that, actually, he had invited more people and that Tina had decided she wanted to wear a dress. Since she did not have an appropriate dress in her wardrobe, I told him that as soon as they arrived Saturday morning, she and I would go shopping.

At exactly eleven A.M., my son and his future wife arrived. I was ready, list in hand, to begin our marathon day. This left me eight whole hours . . . Before we headed to the nearest town to find Tina a dress, we picked up the wedding cake and the bouquet and left them in the refrigerator at my parents' house.

We had to drive forty-five miles to the nearest suitable dress shops. At a resale shop, we were shocked to see the price tags on the secondhand gowns—the least expensive dress was $250. Tina, who did not want to spend that kind of money, refused to try any of them on. The dress was to be a gift from me, but she did not want me to spend that kind of money, either.

At the next shop, we found some simple but suitable gowns for the occasion. After trying on several dresses, Tina, who is not a frills-and-lace type, decided on a simple ivory one that flattered her long dark hair and her figure. After selecting appropriate undergarments and jewelry, we left the shop, pleased that we had spent less than the $250 for the other dress. Now, for the shoes. All she needed to complete the outfit was shoes.

It was two P.M. and we still had shopping to do for the reception. We literally raced down the street to a shoe shop, but Tina could not find a pair to fit. Thinking that my mother wore the same size as Tina, I called her on my cell phone to find out if she had a pair of ivory or bone dress shoes. She did, but they were a half size smaller than Tina's.

"I can squeeze my feet into them for the ceremony." Tina shrugged when I told her the size. "It won't last that long."

"But you also have the reception," I said. "Let's stop back by the resale shop on the way home and see if we can find you a pair." We were in luck. For $9 we found a pair of ivory satin pumps; although they weren't made of glass, they fit as if they had been made for Cinderella. Another problem solved!

We made one more stop before we returned to the house to get ready. At the local Super Wal-Mart store—what would we do without it?—we grabbed a cart and barreled through the store, tossing paper plates, napkins, silverware, cups, peanuts, mints, and other items for the reception into it. We decided to serve soda pop. Who had time to mess with punch?

The clock struck four as we ran into the house. We all took showers, fixed our hair, and hollered at the males in the household —who *never* sweat the small stuff—to start getting ready.

By five P.M.—two hours before the ceremony—Tina and I were dressed and ready to head to the Methodist church at Chelsea. The drive was an hour, which would put us at the church exactly one hour before the ceremony. We left before Casey, his brother, and their father, so we could get things ready for the reception. We still had to stop at my parents' house to pick up the cake and Tina's bouquet. We didn't even worry about decorating the church. Time was of the essence. We had a wedding ceremony to pull off.

The nuptials did not begin promptly at seven as planned; the groom and his best man, my youngest son, were running late. It didn't matter—the hastily planned celebration was moving forward at its own pace. It had taken on a life of its own.

The simple but moving ceremony was highlighted with humor when the best man pretended to have misplaced the plain gold bands the couple had chosen. Casey looked like he was ready to strangle his younger brother, but the congregation laughed when Reverend Smith—who had been in on the joke—said, "Clint, we really had them going there for a minute, didn't we?"

The reception that followed was as joyful as the ceremony that celebrated the marriage of two young people who had chosen a simple beginning for their future together.

How did this mother, who used to get stressed out when one of her sons put off his homework until the last minute, pull off a church wedding in five days? It was simple—I realized that the happiness of the couple was the most important factor. It didn't matter that there were no fancy invitations or three-layer cake, or that the groom's mother was also the official wedding photographer. I realized that if I could put a wedding together at such short notice, I could handle anything.

—*Carol A. Round*

This Is the Way
We Go to School

I have heard the horror stories of that oft-anticipated-yet-dreaded first day on the pathway to cap and gown: moms and dads ripping themselves away from their screaming children, then melting down into pathetic puddles of guilt or, possibly even worse, parents being summarily dismissed with a casual wave at the classroom door, then collapsing under the conflicting feelings of relief and rejection. By far the most positive tale was that of some friends of mine whose kids all started school together. These mothers bought a bottle of champagne and floated on happy bubbles for three hours.

I wanted to be a floater, too—not a melter or a collapser. But I worried that preschool might not work out for us at all this year. As ready as Kayla was, often slipping her arms through her diaper bag handles to pretend she had a school knapsack, her health refused to cooperate, knocking her on her potty-trained butt.

After a week in the hospital with viral *and* bacterial pneumonia (hey, my baby doesn't do anything halfway) and reactive respiratory disease (better known to the lay population—myself included—as asthma), she had had several "reactive respiratory disease incidents," and we were still in the midst of experimenting with the menu of treatment options. ("Will that be hyperactivity or super-sensitivity with your macaroni today, miss?") Her moods fluctuated dramatically. First she would be excited, pretending to do homework with pencil and paper; then she'd regress to that death-grip-around-the-knees stage (also known as the Klingon stage, but more technically referred to as "separation anxiety"). But Kayla wanted to go to school, and I wanted her to adjust gradually to the more structured schedule that would be required in a couple of years, so I had enrolled her for Tuesday and Thursday mornings.

Overkill being my personal style, I prepared meticulously. I read her to sleep with books about starting preschool. I used every opportunity available to familiarize Kayla with the new environment: I took her along on the tour, and Sam came from work to meet us on visiting day so Kayla could show him where the dress-up clothes were and introduce him to her teacher. And for a couple of weeks, I woke Kayla up earlier every day to adjust her sleep schedule so we wouldn't have to rush in the mornings.

On Preschool Eve, after Kayla was in bed, I packed the real backpack my mom had made for this momentous occasion, complete with her granddaughter's name in glittery gold puff paint. I realized this was a task I would probably be doing for years to come. Strains of "Sunrise, Sunset" echoed through my mind. Today it was a change of clothes in case of an "accident"; tomorrow it would be lunch money and field trip permission slips—until I'm banned from touching her stuff at all, that is.

I wondered how Kayla would take to preschool. Her parting style would determine how I would spend my three hours. Would I treat myself to brunch at my favorite restaurant, lingering over roast hazelnut cream coffee while enriching my mind with a popular magazine? I threw a year-old magazine into my shoulder pack. Or would I park across the street from the school and sob over the steering wheel until the double doors swung open to reunite me with my only child? I added a box of tissues to the tote bag.

Because we'd have to do a time-consuming breathing treatment before leaving in the morning, I decided our preparation would be more relaxed and efficient if Kayla ate breakfast during our thirty-minute drive into town. I added a container of dry cereal to the pile, put a sippy cup of apple juice in the refrigerator, and taped a note to the door—"Take juice." Then, for the first time since Kayla had been born, I set the alarm clock.

When I whispered, "Good morning, sugar pie," to wake her, Kayla's eyes popped open, and her bottom lip quivered. "Mama, I don't want to go to school. I'm too little."

I spent lots of time saying the appropriate Mommy things: "It's okay to be scared . . . I was scared, too . . . loved it . . . made lots of new friends." She countered, "But I want my *old* friends to be there."

I told her going to school was all part of growing up, like going to movies and getting a bicycle.

She pondered this for a moment. *Aha,* I thought. *Now I've got her.* But she crossed her arms over her chest, lowered her chin, and said in an ominously quiet voice, "I not going to grow up. I have nothing to do with it."

Although Sam had already gone to work, I could hear him cheering in my mind. He had been a non-growth advocate since the day we took down Kayla's crib, and often told me to stop feeding her and teaching her things so she'd stop growing up. Personally, though, I couldn't suppress a chuckle in response to her earnest stance.

So she said it three more times, grinning when I responded with more laughter.

Taking advantage of our good humor, I reminded her what to expect at school, reciting as fast as I could: "Free Time to play with toys, Circle Time for stories and lessons, Snack Time for yummy in the tummy, Center Time for art and other projects, Music Time, Outdoor Time for sandbox and slide, then Mommy-pick-you-up-and-take-you-out-to-lunch-so-you-can-tell-me-all-about-it time." Giggles from her and then the all-important nod.

After getting dressed and using the respirator while watching Barney, we marched out to the car, singing "This is the way we go to school, go to school, go to school . . ." I buckled Kayla into her car seat, then reached for my purse, which I keep under the front seat.

But my purse wasn't there this morning and I realized instantly that it was still in Sam's car from when we'd gone out to dinner the night before. While my car remained in place, my mind accelerated into overdrive: *Okay, okay, don't panic, you've got a spare key somewhere. Where is it? Oh, right here in my shoulder bag, gosh, this is your lucky day. You've got no money or license, but there's gas in the tank. Just drive to school—don't speed; then drive right to Sam's office for your purse. Now take a deep breath; picture yourself on the mossy bank of a babbling brook; and drive already.*

I started the car, reversed down the driveway, then got out to open the gate. Ack, it was locked! Sam had secured the padlock when he went to work. I did not have an extra key to that. *Mossy bank, babbling brook, come back. Okay, still no need to panic, we'll just be late, that's all.* I got Kayla, still singing ("...go to school, early Tuesday morning"), out of her car seat, called our neighbor who does have our spare gate key on the off chance that he was home sick from work. He wasn't, dang his good health. Then I called Sam, who was in the middle of a quality assurance inspection and could not leave.

The thought to ask a friend to pick up my keys and drive them out entered my mind but was immediately dismissed. That would take too long. When a vision of me hoisting Kayla onto my back and scaling the six-foot fence to presumably borrow a neighbor's car formed, reality sank in. *Give it up—this ain't happening.*

Back to the original question of how I would handle Kayla's first day of school. Did I cry? You bet I did. But after I called in (making a powerful first impression as the ditzy mother who was locked in her own yard) and heard in the background at least half the school emoting like a batch of mourners at Elmo's funeral, I was relieved to put off for two more days our potentially traumatic parting.

While I unloaded the backpack, juice, and cereal from the car, Kayla did a happy dance in the driveway, singing "This is the way we stay at home, stay at home, stay at home. . . ."

I climbed onto the car hood to watch her celebration. Me, I didn't feel much like champagne, but I twisted the lid off the apple juice and lifted the purple cup in a silent toast to her celebration. After all, there was always Thursday, our *next* first day of preschool.

—*April Burk*

The Best Part of the Day

Hold fast to the good. That phrase stuck in my mind for years before I put it to use in my children's bedtime ritual. After I decided to resign from the corporate world in order to spend more time with my children, life took on new meaning. I used to race from work to the grocery store, hauling my children from one place to another. My guide was my wristwatch; my connections came from cell phones and e-mail. I even raced through reading books to my children at night, secretly making mental lists in my head of all the other things I had to achieve before I went to bed. After making the decision to stay home with my children, I found more time to reflect on my choices. I wondered if all those years I had been truly living in the moment.

And so began "the best part of our day," a nightly ritual that allows my children and me to stop and reflect on the good in each day. Nightly, without fail, as I arrange the covers around each child, I quietly ask, "What was the best part of your day?" They are always quick to answer and they always reply with a smile. One night, my son surprised me and asked the same question of me: "What was the best part of your day, Mommy?" I have to honestly admit that it took much more time for me to stop, breathe, and reflect on the good in my day. Some nights it is hard to find an answer, but this ritual has forced me to face my own day in a different way.

I used to tuck my children in bed, then flop on the couch with my husband for an hour of grumbling about my day. Now, I think, "What happened today that I treasure as the best part?" I enjoy the simplest moments the most: holding hands with my children on a walk, watching my son's basketball game, or doing a puzzle with my daughter. The simple acts, not the big things.

By reflecting each night on our best moments, we are reaffirming our focus on the successes of the day instead of the failures. As a parent, I can listen carefully to what is important to my children. I learn a great deal during these moments. The small gestures that I think are not important to them are often the very moments they single out as the best ones. Sometimes I receive a pleasant surprise. What they say is the best part of their day is a disguised expression of gratitude to me. Not once in the year we have been doing our nightly ritual have my children ever said the best part of the day had anything to do with a material object. The best part of their days have always been "catching fireflies" or "riding my bike really fast down the sidewalk" or even "when I came home after school and you were waiting for me on the front porch." Moments like that truly affirm my decision to stay home, to be there on that front porch.

There are days when we all struggle to find meaning in our lives. Seeking out the best part of a day allows us to remember that the simplest gestures are often the most meaningful. And so in this nightly ritual, we all have learned that the troubles of the day cannot defeat us. It has taught us to stop and take notice, but most important, to celebrate the day. That is what life is all about.

—*Vicky DeCoster*

Bryan's Story

Bryan hurried into this world on August 22, 1984. He arrived on the first day of school as I was beginning a new teaching year with a class of kindergarten children. My first day on the job did not go at all as planned—after only one hour of being with my newly arrived five-year-old students, I was whisked off to the hospital.

A few hours later Bryan was born, weighing four pounds and thirteen ounces. Bryan was born a month premature and spent seven days in intensive care. While he was hospitalized, the medical team discovered that Bryan had apnea. The pediatrician described it as a sleep disorder where the baby basically forgets to breathe. Bryan came home weighing four pounds and seven ounces and with a heart monitor apparatus. My husband and I were trained in infant CPR, the attachment of electrodes to Bryan's body, and the meaning of the beeps of the monitor. We were to never be more than forty-five seconds away from the baby while he was sleeping. Needless to say, my kindergarten students didn't see me back on the job for many, many months.

Premature babies often have health difficulties. Bryan was no exception. When he was young, he continually had ear infections. We discovered more hospital emergency rooms over numerous Christmas breaks than most people do in a lifetime as we attempted visits to grandparents and relatives in other states during the holidays. Bryan became very good at self-diagnosing his ear infections. He could tell me when it was time to go to the doctor, and 95 percent of the time he called it correctly. Three sets of ear tubes and five years later, Bryan made it through this phase.

Once we passed through the ear infection stage, though, another challenge arose. During a routine check by the school nurse of all fifth graders at Bryan's elementary school, it was discovered that Bryan had scoliosis, an abnormal curvature of the spine. We knew this had to be monitored by an orthopedic specialist, since Bryan's older brother had also been diagnosed at this same age. Scoliosis is usually a malady that affects girls, so it was very unusual that both our boys ended up with this diagnosis.

And so began an annual routine of doctor's visits to X-ray and monitor the situation. The X-rays usually showed a slight curve, which was of no worry to the specialist at this time.

The year that Bryan's curve changed, though, threw us all for a loop. At his annual checkup with the specialist, his X-rays indicated that the curve had changed from 17 degrees to 38 degrees. This was considered a drastic increase, and we were sent to Iowa City Hospitals to have an orthopedic surgeon examine Bryan.

It was determined at this meeting that Bryan had quite a bit of growing to do yet in his life and the curve could become out of control if it was not directed differently. Bryan was to be fitted and wear an upper body brace for fourteen to eighteen hours each day. Talk about a devastating blow to a thirteen-year-old!

The body brace was quite an impediment. It was designed with Bryan wrapped like a mummy in papier-mâché–like material to create a body mold. When the brace was ready for the final fitting, it was so snug it appeared to be a second skin because the expandable straps had to be pulled extremely tight. This tightness was critical to affect the curvature to any degree. The brace reached from Bryan's hip area to his neck. Bless his heart, though, Bryan never complained during any of this.

The brace really seemed to be working the first two years. The semi-annual visits showed that the curvature had lessened to below 20 degrees. Bryan and the rest of us were thrilled! Our joy did not last long, though: on a routine doctor's visit they discovered a drastic change — 17 degrees to 48 degrees in less than six months. The brace was no longer working for Bryan.

Surgery was recommended by the orthopedic surgeon our family had grown to trust. We talked, prayed, sought other advice, and decided the surgery had to be done.

On a cold, snowy day in December, Bryan underwent five hours of surgery in which two metal rods (each approximately eighteen inches long) were inserted into his back. These rods are attached to his spine with hooks. They will stay there for his entire life.

Bryan was in the hospital for seven days. I stayed with him the entire time, sleeping on a cot in his room. We had prepared ourselves for the operation, the hospital stay, the six-month recovery period, and his time away from school. We weren't prepared for the amount of pain he would experience throughout his recovery. The only time any of us cried was when he came out of surgery and wondered why we had done this because of the excruciating pain he was experiencing. Otherwise, our son had shown extreme courage in all he had endured previously. In fact, he impressed us with his continual positive attitude.

A year has passed since Bryan's surgery. Of course, he has healed greatly since then. The six-month recovery period seemed to drag on to Bryan, but by the middle of the summer, he was trying a few careful jumps on his skateboard. He has neck pains often, but has grown to accept this, among other things, as part of the healing process.

Just a few weeks ago, Bryan has been telling us that his gums hurt. Wisdom teeth, my husband and I thought. We told him to take some medicine for pain relief, thinking that would be the end of that, but the pain persisted. Sure enough, it's his wisdom teeth—they are coming in horizontally! Each one is impacted and will have to be dug out. The dentist is sure he is also going to have to wear braces once this is completed.

What more could go wrong? I thought, feeling bad for Bryan because I was viewing this as another double whammy that wouldn't be over quickly. Turning to Bryan as we drove home from the dentist, I said, "Bryan, I am so sorry you have to go through all of this."

Bryan looked at me calmly and said, "Mom, are you kidding me? This will be nothing! Remember, I have two rods in my back. Anything after that won't seem so bad."

Putting our troubles into perspective can help us see the more important issues in life. Here is a child who never exhibited any self-pity for his difficulties. Bryan seems to have raised the bar of what the small stuff really is before he considers if it's worth sweating over it. If only the rest of us could do that, we'd find more joy in each day, more pleasure in each encounter. Bryan has taught his family the meaning behind faith, patience, and steadfastness. What a valuable lesson for us all to learn.

— *Diane McCarty*

Rich and Did Not Realize

When I was twelve, I had a bad case of the green-eyed monster disease. In fact, jealousy was an understatement of my feelings toward the kids who actually got to stay at the state park resort, instead of only docking at the resort's marina to get gas. Who were these lucky creatures, leading lives of idle enjoyment while I was stuck being a member of my dorky family?

I enviously eyed balconies decorated with beach towels hanging to dry from a dip in the resort's pool. Delicious smells wafted from the lodge's lakeside café as our pontoon boat headed out to the lake's public beach. How I wished I could be in the pool like the boy I had watched zoom down the pool's slide, instead of swimming in the murky lake with my brothers. Such glamour! Just like the happy families on television shows.

As we ate ham and cheese sandwiches (made at home), fighting ants and sweat bees, I longed to be like the little girl who had been enjoying her meal in peace inside the air-conditioned café. Those children were sitting at tables with real napkins, feasting on the things they chose themselves from a printed menu.

Me? I choked down the sandwich my mother had made hours before, the bread somewhat dried out in the interim. I just knew when *I* was grown, *my* children would be spared this humiliation. Never would they have to watch hungrily from a distance as the cool kids frolicked in splendor. No, I would either make enough money or marry someone who'd made enough money so we could afford to bring our children to the resort.

Recently, my husband and I took our two small children to this same resort. And sure enough, I was true to my childhood vow. My children got to swim in the indoor pool with the slide and later hang their beach towels out on the balcony to dry. No dry homemade sandwiches, either—we enjoyed a delicious dinner at the lodge's air-conditioned lakeside café. It was all wonderful, but I found myself thinking that something was wrong. Something was missing.

That night I lay awake for hours, reliving moments from my childhood in my head, remembering times of laughter and warmth with my parents and my siblings. What a special time it was. Why didn't I feel the same way about this trip? It all seemed so . . . sterile. Too perfect.

I was up early the next day, a woman with a mission. My husband was more than a little startled when I asked him to find me a local grocery store. There were a few things I needed, some bread, some ham, some cheese . . . After making our purchases, I marched my little family troop across the resort lawn and followed the signs to the public beach.

Down at the beach, as I watched my daughter Savannah sifting through the sand hoping to find a treasure such as a shell, listened to son Cameron squeal in delight when another boat made waves crash on the shore, and munched on ham and cheese sandwiches while watching a beautiful sunset on the lake, I finally realized not only what had been missing the previous day of our stay, but also what I had failed to realize at the age of twelve.

All those years I'd imagined that the wealthy were those who stayed indoors at the resort, I was wrong. The truly rich ones those summers at the beach had been my family. We had enjoyed God's priceless gifts of nature's beauty—the way every child (as well as every adult) should—up close and natural. Or in one simple word, outdoors! This vacation with my own family had been an eye-opener. I gained a new perspective on family time together, and a healthy taste for ham and cheese.

—*Stephanie Ray Brown*

The Unanticipated Book

My wife Starlett and I got married right after our graduation from the university, and just as quickly I became an officer in the Army with an obligation to serve for two years.

We were assigned to Alaska. Even though the Army took up most of my time, she and I started working with kids in the base's youth group in our spare time. We loved that experience, and talked often about the prospect of someday having a family of our own.

After a year in Alaska, I was assigned to Vietnam. It meant that Starlett and I were separated for a year, but we managed to maintain the closeness of our marriage by letters and the occasional treat of talking by radiophone. War teaches us many things, most of all how very precious and fragile life is.

But war spared me, and the day finally arrived when I returned home to Starlett. The moment I first saw her face again when we met up in Hawaii will stay fresh in my mind's eye forever.

Life quickly settled down. We moved to San Francisco, I started a career, and a short year later our daughter Courtly was born. When she was born, I remember feeling as though I had already loved her for years. The joy and gratitude were immense. She brought a happiness into our lives that seemed to grow each day.

Two years later, my wife was pregnant again, but now there was concern. I was so in love with my daughter. I had never known that kind of love before, and somehow became convinced that I could never have that amount of love for another child. I wrestled with the guilt as I questioned my capacity to equally love another. Then at midnight in the middle of July, my son Taylor was born. My fears were unfounded. With just one glance at him, everything changed. I discovered within me a whole new love—a love without measure and without limits, just for my new son.

As the months passed, I became increasingly aware of my new capacity to love. My children would do certain things, such as a word, a touch, an expression, and love for them would fill my heart. In their world of simplicity and innocence, I was discovering a joyful and heartfelt capacity to really love. As I realized this, I wanted to share it with each of them . . . but how?

I was consumed by my love for them, yet completely unable to explain to them how very much they were loved. So I decided to write a book and give it to them when they grew up. I wanted them to know how much they were wanted, how much they were loved, and how much they gave me in my life. My decision was to write "in the moment" as much as possible. As I would have experiences with them and feel love for them, I would try to write while still within the emotion of those times. Starting with a blank pad of paper I found in the kitchen, I wrote out my feelings in longhand several times a week for twelve years.

What did I write about all those years? Not about their accomplishments in school or on the playing field. Not about their achievements. I wrote about how it felt to be hugged by them. I wrote about the things we'd done together during the day.

Courtly and Taylor are now grown, and each has married. Neither have children yet, but my daughter is pregnant. I thank them for the book inside of me and the experience of writing it these many years. The book is done, and I plan to have it printed up and give a completed copy to each of them this year.

My children changed my life when they showed me that love abounds and is limitless when the heart is willing. By just being themselves, they have encouraged me, to the extent that I am able, to love generously the people in my life.

—*Clark Stevens*

Very Good advice

Excellent Reading — Read a
second time Aug. 22/2022